Communion Meditations

School of Divinity

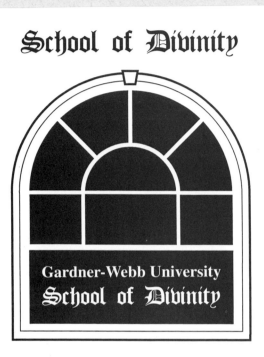

Gardner-Webb University
School of Divinity

This book donated
by

Victor Payne

Communion
Meditations

Edited by

GASTON FOOTE

ABINGDON-COKESBURY PRESS
New York • Nashville

COMMUNION MEDITATIONS

COPYRIGHT MCMLI
BY PIERCE AND SMITH

B

SET UP, PRINTED, AND BOUND BY THE PARTHENON PRESS, AT NASHVILLE, TENNESSEE, UNITED STATES OF AMERICA

Preface

IN MANY OF OUR PROTESTANT CHURCHES THE DEEPER meanings of the Holy Communion have been lost. The observance of this sacrament has too frequently become sterile, perfunctory, ritualistic, and unintelligible. Instituted by Jesus Christ to stimulate and consummate a genuine unity among his followers, it has become the means of accentuating sectarian differences.

It would be useless to assume that the recovery of the meaning of the Holy Communion is the answer to modern Christendom's weakness. But to infer that there is no connection between the low state of our spiritual health and our lackadaisical methods of observing this sacred sacrament is but to be blind to the basic facts of life.

There are two reasons for our apparent desuetude with reference to the Holy Communion. The first is the traditional Protestant revolt against symbolism and the medieval rubrics and liturgies of worship. The reformers emphasized the religion of the spirit and were bitter in their criticism of the Roman Church, whose sacramentarian emphasis had become, at times, a public scandal. But, as is often the case, in their revolt against form, liturgy, and curtsies to idols they threw away much that was of value.

Most of us agree that the worshiping church is both priestly and prophetic in its program. The priest is the representative of man before God. He leads the people in corporate worship and instructs them in the expression of their faith by corporate acts. The prophet is the representative of God before man. He declares to the people the divine will and purpose of the Almighty. The priest preserves the forms of worship; the prophet seeks to purify them. The priest is the conservative; the prophet is the liberal.

Protestantism has consistently emphasized the prophetic nature of religion. It has assumed, and rightly, that Jesus was himself a prophet, a reformer seeking to put new meaning in ancient customs. But the priestly function of religion cannot lightly be tossed aside. Men do need the priest to lead them in meaningful acts of worship. The sacraments of baptism and the Holy Communion are or can be means of grace to our people. Baptism is symbolic of entrance into the Christian fellowship. The Holy Communion is symbolic of the abiding presence of Christ within us. When we Protestants become indifferent to the holy sacraments of the church, we overlook the priestly function of religion, that is, the means of the expression of our corporate faith.

The second reason why the service of Holy Communion is not as spiritually enriching as it ought to be may be in the attitude of the minister himself. When the minister feels no atmosphere of expectancy, no sense of divine Presence, the people are quick to capture his mood. If the minister feels that the observance of the Holy Communion is something to be done because his church periodically demands it, it will become sheer mimicry, void of spiritual power.

As a minister for twenty-five years I have tried to make the service of Holy Communion as meaningful as possible. First of all I have sought to carefully plan every detail of the service—the music, the prayers, the movements of the people, and the moments of silence. To be effective, the service must be orderly and unhurried. To be time-conscious

here is tragic. In the second place I have sought to prepare
the people for the reception of the Holy Communion by
emphasizing some phase of its meaning in a short sermon.
It is precisely because I have had difficulty in finding fresh
homiletic material to enrich the Communion meditations
that this volume is being published. If one is disposed to
saturate his mind and heart in these meditations, he will see
for himself the deeper meaning of the Holy Communion
and thereby transfer his own mood to his communicants.

The time at which the Holy Communion ought to be
observed will vary with the church and the community.
Many of our nonliturgical Protestant churches are providing
a service of Holy Communion in the chapel every Sunday
either before or after the morning sermon. Others are having
special Communion services among smaller groups in the
church sanctuary at stated intervals. Still others who observe
monthly the Holy Communion have it in the morning one
month and in the evening by candlelight the next month.
Those who have sought to enrich this service have not only
elevated its value in the lives of their people but have seen
the rewards in the deepening of their devotional lives.

During Jesus' lifetime he had repeatedly attempted to
prepare his disciples for his death. In those last hours he
took the simple elements of bread and wine, without which
no Judean meal was complete, and made of them symbols
of his last full measure of devotion. He commanded his
disciples, "This do in remembrance of me." How better can
we express our own faith than through remembering him
through life, death, and resurrection? The recurring drama
of commemoration of the Holy Communion can keep alive
the conscience of the Christian community as no other act
of worship. It is our duty as ministers of Jesus Christ to

make this memorial to our Lord so meaningful to our people that it may be for them a never-to-be-forgotten means of grace. If these meditations can deepen the meaning and value of the Holy Communion in the mind of the minister and his people, I am sure the contributors to this volume will feel abundantly repaid for their efforts.

GASTON FOOTE

Contents

Communion Meditations

What the Communion Service Means

ROBERT J. McCRACKEN

THE COMMUNION SERVICE IS THE CENTRAL ACT OF WOR-
ship of the Christian Church. Of all the means of grace it
is indubitably the chief. By no other avenue does God draw
so near to our souls. The brooding silence, the hush that
falls upon the spirit, the sense that the unseen world is very
real and very near—nowhere else in anything like the same
degree are we aware of these things. One who attended a
Communion service afterward wrote: "Sunday was for me a
high-water mark in worship. I seemed to be within touching
distance of God."

The Communion service is the Christian gospel expressed
in symbolic acts. Goethe said that the highest cannot be
spoken. There are truths too profound to put into words
or music. To body forth their meaning we fall back, as
untold generations have done, on the use of symbols—the
handshake which, whether in joy or sorrow, conveys more
than language ever can; the national flag, the sight of which
can put fire into the blood; the wedding ring, the silent,
eloquent token that its wearer has entered into a relationship
which nothing can sever. So the Church takes bread, and
breaks it, and remembers a body that was broken; takes
wine, and pours it out, and remembers the blood that was
shed.

This it does at the bidding of Christ. He instituted the
Communion service. If from the beginning down to the

present time Christendom has held it sacred, it is because it was the last thing he asked of his friends. "This do," he said, "in remembrance of me." He knew our nature. At best our memories are short.

> The evil that men do lives after them,
> The good is oft interred with their bones.

He knew that even our remembrance of him would fade unless it was repeatedly refreshed, refreshed not alone by recollection but by an appeal to our senses, to sight and touch and taste. At his request we take the bread and the wine, for us the holiest symbols in the world; we recall the love wherewith the Saviour loved us and gave himself for us; and as we do, faith is nourished, hope is kindled, strength is renewed. Matthew Arnold in his poem "East London" has given us a description of a walk he took:

> 'Twas August, and the fierce sun overhead
> Smote on the squalid streets of Bethnal Green,
> And the pale weaver, through his windows seen
> In Spitalfields, look'd thrice dispirited.

> I met a preacher there I knew, and said:
> "Ill and o'er-worked, how fare you in this scene?"—
> "Bravely!" said he; "for I of late have been
> Much cheered with thoughts of Christ, *the living bread*."

For nineteen hundred years that has been the authentic Christian experience. It is the story of hundreds today.

It explains another aspect of the Communion service. It is a service of thanksgiving as well as of remembrance. For this reason some speak of it as the Eucharist. Here we give grateful praise in hymn and prayer for all that Christ has brought us—peace with God, the forgiveness of sins, power to break free from our sins. "All my life," wrote

Seneca, "I have been seeking to climb out of the pit of my besetting sins. And I can't do it: and I never will, unless a hand is let down to draw me up." The hand, thank God, has been let down. Power is available to live victoriously. No one need live a beaten life. Christ conquers besetting sin, reclaims us to character and power, remembers us when we forget him, believes in us when we lose faith in ourselves, heartens and empowers us to try again and again and again. Is it any wonder that those who have availed themselves of his saviorhood should say when they come to his table, "Bless the Lord, O my soul, and forget not all his benefits"?

A service of remembrance! A service of thanksgiving! It is also a service of communion. Brother Lawrence said that the time of prayer did not with him differ from the time of business and that in the noise and clatter of the monastery kitchen, while several persons were at the same time calling for different things, he possessed God in as great tranquillity as if he were on his knees at the blessed Sacrament. He found it possible by dint of arduous and sustained self-discipline to commune with God anywhere.

After the famous British surgeon Lord Moynihaum had performed an operation before a group of fellow surgeons, someone asked him how he could possibly do what he did with such a crowd around him. "Well," he said, "it is like this: there are just three people in the theater when I operate—the patient and I."

"Three?" said his friend. "But that is only two. Who is the other?"

And the surgeon answered, "God."

Some have been able to offer the same testimony. In the home, on the street, at their work they have known the presence of God. With the majority of us those have been rare and fleeting experiences, standing out in memory like mountain peaks. It is when we receive the bread and the wine that God comes closest to us, comes to us in Christ and makes himself real to our faith. What begins as a memorial becomes a presence.

Our fellowship is not only with God but with one another. John Wesley liked to say that there is no such thing as a solitary Christian. The Christian life is not an isolated life but a community life. And nowhere is the sense of community as strong or as deep as at the Lord's Table. Here we meet on common ground. Here all barriers of race and color and class and circumstance are abolished. There is nothing in history comparable to the unbroken observance, in ever-widening ranges of language and race, of the breaking of the bread and the taking of the cup in remembrance of the death of Jesus. Think of the millions who have gathered or will gather in obedience to Christ's last command—by land and by sea, in ancient cathedrals and simple chapels, in churches Roman Catholic, Anglican, Baptist, Congregationalist, Lutheran, Methodist, Presbyterian, and Reformed. Here we are one. The distinctions that obtain elsewhere are forgotten. This is the heart and climax of the worship of the Church. In the fact of Christ there is far more to unite us than there can be anywhere else to divide us.

Another note should run through this service. Remembrance, thanksgiving, communion, and dedication. We speak of the Sacrament of the Lord's Supper. The word "sacrament" comes from a Latin word meaning the pledge or vow of loyalty and allegiance taken by a soldier to his leader. From the beginning as Christians have received the sacred elements they have made vows—to amend and improve their ways, to live after the example and spirit of Christ, to put God before Mammon, service before self,

love before hate. Such resolves sweep over us when
we think of Christ and his Cross. We are ashamed that
we have not caught the infection of his great spirit—
that our prayers are so cold, our lives are so self-centered,
the range of our vision is so narrow. But we are not without
the desire to catch the infection. We want to have done
with weakness and self-indulgence, and to rededicate ourselves to him. We want him to be the center around which
everything else turns. And when we receive the bread and
the wine, we ask for grace to make him, with no "ifs" or
"buts," with no conditions or reservations, Master and Lord
of our lives.

The Implications in the Memorial Meal

EDWARD H. PRUDEN

And when the hour was come, he sat down, and the twelve apostles with him.   —Luke 22:14

IN ADDITION TO THE MORE OBVIOUS TRUTHS WHICH ARE contained in the institution of the Lord's Supper, there are a number of significant spiritual implications in the celebration of this memorial meal which the Christian should recognize. Within the scope of these pages it would be impossible to mention all of them, but I shall list at least five.

First of all there is the implication that every Christian needs the ministry of a quiet place. When the Lord came to the point in his ministry when he desired to inaugurate this meal which would serve as a memorial to him and a reminder of the spiritual implications of his death, he directed his disciples to an upper room, presumably a place of quiet detachment removed from the noise of the streets and the interruptions of the multitude. There is no doubt that this was an ideal setting for the institution of his memorial, but one suspects there is in the selection of that place at least a suggestion to the follower of Christ that to such a place every sincere soul should repair at frequent intervals.

Our Protestant Christianity has impressed the world with its boundless energy and its businesslike administration of its affairs. However, one wonders just how successful we have been in impressing upon the minds of people the necessity for meditation and prayer. While our ceaseless activity has unquestionably achieved a great deal, it is altogether possible that much more could have been done if such activity has been interspersed with a reasonable number of quiet periods in which the soul was brought face to face with God.

In an age of much mechanical noise and moral confusion we are all the more in need of those secret places where the interruptions of a highly technical civilization are momentarily shut out and the spirit of man is given an opportunity to commune with the God who made it. More and more is being demanded of the Christian by way of demonstrating his discipleship, and all of this emphasizes the need for storing up within oneself those adequate resources which come only from God. Some of us have learned from bitter experiences that these resources do not come to us in the ordinary avenues of life but only when we deliberately draw away from the many demands of an average existence and observe a quiet time for meditation and prayer.

A second implication in the memorial meal is the need for Christian fellowship. In that upper room in Jerusalem long ago there gathered a group of individuals who had come to mean a great deal to each other and who were destined to mean a great deal to the Kingdom of God. With the exception of Judas Iscariot there had grown up between the disciples and their Leader a great bond of confidence and affection. Much of what they had already been able to achieve, and were later to accomplish, grew out of that fellowship which had come to mean so much in their own personal experience. Outside those four walls there prevailed many antagonizing forces and discordant voices, but within that little room there was, at least for a time, a harmony of spirit and a unity of purpose which must have been tremendously rewarding and encouraging.

Every pastor with even a minimum of experience as the leader of a church has discovered how indispensable is the experience of fellowship in a Christian's growth and development. Many of those who become lost to the church and ultimately have their names placed on inactive lists lose the contact with fellow believers that keeps the spiritual light aglow in the lives of many; and when this experience is lacking, many drift away into loneliness, discouragement, and despair. In larger cities particularly, where mutitudes are away from home and loved ones, the church has a tremendous responsibility in making the house of God a spiritual home for its members. In such churches many discover the truthfulness of those words in the old hymn:

> The fellowship of kindred minds
> Is like to that above.

A third implication in the memorial meal is the Christian's world task. In partaking of the simple articles of food and drink which were a part of the everyday diet of all men, the disciples were reminded that the ideals and truths which Jesus had shared with them were as needful to life at its best as food and drink are to bodily existence, and in turn were to be shared with all men. They had not been selected through any divine favoritism in order that they might personally enjoy a secret which was to be concealed from all the rest of humanity, but were rather the recipients of a message which in due season was to be published abroad.

While the teachings of some other religions make certain helpful contributions to the life of individuals in certain areas of the world and in certain eras of history, it can be said without the slightest bigotry that the message of Christ is the only faith which is both universal and timeless in its appeal. Every man discovers in the gospel of Christ something which seems to have been placed there particularly for his own personal need, and its implications are just as applicable in an Oriental environment as in an Occidental. The missionary responsibilities of the Christian Church are inescapable, and the branches of the Christian Church which have been most sacrificial and influential in promoting the missionary task have been those branches which have experienced the greatest growth and realized the most dynamic vitality.

This world mission has become even more compelling in recent years as the realization has grown that the whole cause of world peace is inseparably related to this program of ours for evangelizing the nations. In former years we have more or less depended upon the growing sense of horror of war and the increased efforts to establish some international machinery to promote the cause of peace. Now there is beginning to dawn upon us the rather startling fact that peace will become possible only when there is a disposition within the human spirit toward brotherhood and good will. This disposition, however, is not a thing with which men are born, nor does it develop as a natural process of physical growth and mental expansion. It comes as a direct result of a spiritual experience with Christ which impresses upon the individual his inescapable relationship to all other men, and which designates this relationship as brotherhood.

Another implication in the Lord's Supper is a sense of dependence. No thoughtful person who sits around a table partaking of the food which nourishes life and produces energy can ever ignore the extent to which he is dependent upon those who have planted, cultivated, and harvested the crops, as well as his dependence upon the God who produces the soil, the sunshine, and the rain. Our modern civilization has become so efficient in producing the necessities of life at the smallest expenditure of energy that we are sometimes inclined to lose sight of the factors which have gone into the production and distribution of these blessings. As I was rushing out of my front door recently to meet an urgent engagement, I suddenly caught sight of the bottles of milk which had been left on the front porch a few moments before by the milkman. With some irritation I paused long enough in my haste to pick up the bottles of milk and take them inside to the icebox, feeling a bit annoyed that I had to have my regular schedule so rudely interrupted. Later on as I drove from my home to my office, I felt a bit ashamed of myself when I remembered the ease with which milk now comes to my own table as compared with the experiences which my father and grandfather must have known.

We do not pause often enough amidst life's mad rush to recognize how much is being done for us by others—those unseen hands which F. W. Boreham has referred to in his essay concerning those who held the ropes at the top of the Damascus wall while Paul was being lowered in safety on the other side. And of course the Christian in particular needs to remember his absolute dependence upon the wisdom and power of God. To his hands has been committed a task which requires far more than human energy and ingenuity. He has been called upon to live a life and render a service which requires all the spiritual strength it is possible for him to absorb.

Finally it should be pointed out that the memorial meal unquestionably suggests the principle of spiritual growth. Just as the body develops in response to the food it partakes, so does the soul of man expand in response to the spiritual resources it receives from the living God. One of the most disturbing features of the experience of many professing Christians is the lack of awareness that discipleship should be a matter of growth. There are entirely too many who feel that having made a public confession of their faith and united with some well-established church, they can then relax, assuming that all vital matters have been attended to. They forget that being a genuine Christian is one of the most difficult tasks imaginable and that even a long life amidst the most ideal influences is insufficient to produce the kind of person we should be in view of our opportunities and responsibilities.

Simon Peter did not find it very difficult to accept Christ as the long-promised Messiah, and it was he who spoke rather eloquently for the other disciples regarding this matter. Peter did find it difficult, however, to adjust his life to the various implications of the message of Christ, and again and again had to be reminded of his difficulties along these lines. In other words, Peter had no difficulty accepting the person of Christ, but he had a world of trouble in adopting the program of Christ. While most of us may not be aware that this is our own personal difficulty, nevertheless such is the case. We underestimate the task of being a Christian, and we neglect to engage in those exercises and disciplines which produce Christian growth. We are too satisfied with ordinary achievements, and we are inclined to find a way of escape from the challenge of a more adventurous Christianity. Partaking of the memorial meal at regular intervals should remind us of the folly of spending so much of our time in activities which have to do with physical growth while neglecting so shamefully those experiences in life which enlarge the spirit and increase our capacity to serve Christ in an acceptable fashion.

The Service of Symbols

W. E. SANGSTER

This do in remembrance of me.—Luke 22:19

It is impossible to cut symbolism out of life. Its roots run deep. If a man were to resolve never to use a symbol again, he could not shake hands with a friend, kiss his child, raise his hat to a lady, display or salute his country's flag; for all of these are symbols. They are meaningless in themselves and intelligible only as the meaning behind them is understood.

Human nature demands symbols. We live in a material world and are able to express ourselves only through material forms. The human heart, in varying degrees, craves some tangible expression of the movements of the spirit; it seeks to cast into a physical mold, if just for a moment, emotions which belong by nature only to the unseen realm. It is an attempt to view the invisible and touch the intangible.

By what means the various common symbols took the form they now possess is an interesting study but one which is beside my present purpose. I am simply seeking to show that symbolism is a natural expression of the human mind and one which may be turned to great use. For instance, it is almost impossible for the human mind to realize nationality apart from its symbol in a flag. Try to conjure up in your own mind what the United States or the British empire would mean to you apart from the Stars and Stripes or the

Union Jack. The clearest ideas you can reach are vague and unreal; the mystic "something" which binds it all together defies description and analysis, yet somehow the flag makes it concrete to the mind.

I once knew an old schoolmaster in London who walked into his classroom every morning and solemnly saluted the Union Jack. It was only a bit of bunting, but in the course of time the boys who watched his simple ritual came to realize that he wasn't really saluting the colored rag but the spirit of loyalty and oneness the flag expressed.

Behind the symbol one must constantly seek the spirit, and behind the form the life that form aims to portray. A symbol so used and so understood may be of incalculable benefit to a human soul.

Oscar Wilde tells in his book *De Profundis* that when he was brought between two policemen from prison to the Court of Bankruptcy, a friend of his waited for him in the long dreary corridor. Before the crowd of eager sight-seers the friend gravely raised his hat to him as, handcuffed and with bowed head, he passed on his shameful way. It was only a symbol, but Wilde adds that it hushed the whole crowd into silence. Later he says, speaking of his life in prison: "When wisdom has been profitless to me, philosophy barren, and the proverbs and phrases of those who have sought to give me consolation as dust and ashes in my mouth, the memory of that little, lovely, silent act of love has unsealed for me all the wells of pity." It was only a symbol, but the symbol lovingly offered and intelligently understood was the one light he saw in the midnight darkness of his remorse.

Moreover, a symbol properly used may nourish and nurture the experience which lies behind it. We teach little boys to raise their hats as a sign of respect. The raising of the hat is only a sign, but few people doubt that it has a salutary effect on the boy's mind and deepens the sense of respect. When two friends meet and greet each other with a hearty handshake, there is in it something more than the observance of an age-long custom. The right hand of fellowship has its own unconscious influence in nourishing the friendship which first prompted the act. A flag, as we have seen, is the symbolic expression of a nation's mystic life; yet the symbol itself does much to warm and deepen national sentiment. The very sight of the flag is enough to stir the hearts of thousands of men and women, and their national loyalty increases as it is stirred. Naval and military commanders know how to use the power of the national symbol. History records many instances of sailors of various nationalities breaking into cheers when their flag was hoisted for action. Nelson sailed into Aboukir Bay with six colors flying, so that even if five were shot away his men would not lose the inspiration of their flag. They were only symbols, but symbols with power to nurture and sustain the spirit they expressed.

The story has often been told of an English sailor who went ashore from his ship at a foreign port, got drunk, and was wrongfully arrested on the supposition that he was involved in a shooting affray. He was condemned to be executed by shooting. The British consul protested at the sheer injustice of it but, failing to have the case retried, asked permission to be present at the execution. He went with a Union Jack in his pocket. When the firing squad marched out and took up position, the consul ran forward and flung his flag across the condemned man and said, "Shoot if you dare." It would have been an act of war to shoot upon the flag. The bunting itself could not have repelled the piercing bullet, but what it stood for was enough. The case was reheard and the man acquitted. Symbols are powerful. They can repel an armor-piercing bullet.

The reverse also is true. Not only does a symbol nourish the experience it expresses, but a symbol omitted may issue in loss. If no fitting expression is found for a fine feeling, the feeling may lose its vitality and die. I knew a home where the father's intensely reserved nature could not abide any expression of love. He neither kissed his children nor allowed them to kiss him. He was a good father, but somehow this firm prohibition became a barrier which grew breast high until at last father and children seemed to be living on opposite sides of a wall. It was only a symbol neglected, a small thing, perhaps, in itself; but it froze the expanding love of those children's hearts, and that father would have given a great deal afterward to drag the barrier down. A symbol neglected may weaken the emotion it was intended to express.

But I fancy I hear someone say: "Symbols are liable to great abuse and can be used only with grave danger." I admit it. I am not unmindful that Judas betrayed his Master with a kiss. I know that the presence of a symbol in no way guarantees the presence of the experience it was designed to express. Men shake hands carelessly with men for whom they have no real regard. Women sometimes kiss one another out of dull convention, though their hearts may be far from warm with affection. These are symbols abused and empty.

In 1930 I went to a great meeting marking the 150th anniversary of the founding of the first Sunday school in the city of Gloucester by Robert Raikes. A large number of ministers were present on the platform. One of them, sitting in front of me, had a gold cross on his watch chain. Imagine my horror to notice him during the speaker's address absentmindedly use the corner of the cross to clean his fingernails. I turned sick inside me and looked away. To such awful abuse can the most solemn symbols be turned by men from whom familiarity has stolen all reverence.

Nevertheless, we are not faced with the question of symbols or no symbols, for life is always forcing them upon us, but rather what wise and restrained use of symbols will best serve us on our pilgrim way.

The history of religion, especially, provides us with many instances of the abuse of symbols; and we must be always on our guard lest outward signs become a substitute for, rather than an expression of, an inward and spiritual grace. It is better to restrict our use of a symbol severely than to use it so often that it becomes nothing but a form.

Having found that symbols are common to all branches of life, we should not be surprised to find them in religion too. Carefully used and jealously guarded, they have their place. The chief symbolic act in the Christian religion has been, and will always remain, the Lord's Supper: the bread as a symbol of his broken body and the wine of his spilled blood. It must take precedence over all other symbolism— the baptismal water apart—because it was instituted by Christ himself. He said, "This do in remembrance of me," and our heart responds,

> This will I do, my dying Lord,
> I will remember Thee.

We may use some symbols of human invention simply because they help us, and some others as the legacy of the race, but that symbol which our Lord proffered among his last acts upon earth should ever hold a chief place in our hearts. It has been held with great reverence by his disciples through the ages.

Observed in different ways and sustained by differences in belief, these symbols of bread and wine have done what symbols are intended to do. They have nourished and nurtured the experience they aimed to express. By the help of "these creatures of bread and wine" the unseen Lord has drawn near and the "real presence" has been given. The weary and sin-stained and disappointed and despairing have touched the hem of his garment and felt his hand upon their heads. The symbolism has helped to deepen their faith and sweeten their lives; it has soothed and comforted and made strong.

We feel ourselves especially fortunate in that the table of the Lord is spread in our midst and the word of welcome invitation is given. We will not neglect the symbol lest the experience it expresses wither and die. We will not treat the solemn feast as a kind of doll's tea party with little chips of bread and little tots of wine. We will recognize that the symbols can have meaning only if we go from the table to our daily toil determined to break ourselves in the service of others and pour out our lifeblood for the triumph of Christ's cause. We will carefully prepare our heart for the reception of the sacrament, therefore, lest it become an empty symbol from which the life and meaning have faded.

The Lord's Countersign

RALPH W. SOCKMAN

IN THE MARRIAGE SERVICE OF MY DENOMINATION THERE comes a point where the ring is about to be placed on the finger of the bride, and sometimes of the groom also. The ring is handed to the minister who blesses it with the words: "The wedding ring is the outward and visible sign of an inward and spiritual bond which unites two loyal hearts in endless love." Such a symbol may seem unnecessary to a cold-blooded, matter-of-fact mind. In fact the marriage ceremony itself may seem a needless yielding to sentimentality. Some may say that marriage is merely a social contract in which two people agree to live together. For the sake of social stability and property rights let the agreement be registered. Isn't that all that is necessary? Why the ceremony of vows and rings and altars? Because life is more than a cold-blooded, matter-of-fact business. Life is a blending of facts and dreams, of cold blood and hot blood. Marriage is a union for better, for worse, for richer, for poorer, in sickness and in health. And, therefore, in our high moods we make vows and use symbols which help to sustain us in our lower moods. Symbols, ceremonies, and anniversaries serve to reinforce love and hold families together.

So is it in the life of nations. When these American colonies began to realize the need of union in their effort to redress the wrongs suffered at the hands of their mother country, the colonists sent delegates to a Continental

Congress, they passed a Declaration of Independence, they adopted Articles of Confederation, and finally a Federal Constitution. Thus they had signed agreements in black and white. Were not these enough? No, people are not inspired and sustained merely by documents in black and white. On January 2, 1776, at Cambridge, Massachusetts, Washington displayed a flag of thirteen stripes with the Union Jack— from which evolved about a year later the flag of these United States with its stars and stripes. Our flag is only a piece of colored cloth! Yet who can measure the influence of that emblem as school children stand to salute it and as citizens turn to gaze at it as they sing our national anthem? What would happen to our morale if we removed all symbols, all shrines, all monuments from our national scene? Why does the British Commonwealth of Nations feel it so important to have a king, surrounded by those historic symbols which quicken the imagination and warm the hearts of the trapper in Saskatchewan and the farmer in South Africa? It is because men need outward and visible symbols and inward and spiritual bonds. Symbols, ceremonies, and anniversaries deliver us from the dead monotony of existence as mountains lift a landscape from wearing levelness into interesting peaks which catch the first glints of the dawn and hold the last lingering rays of the setting sun. Some years ago my own son, then a schoolboy of sixteen, wrote in a class poem these words:

Living's tiny land is mostly plains,
And ecstasy's swift-sinking mountains few and far between.

Yes, life needs its soul-stirring hours and red-letter days to lift us out of our rutted roads, and then we preserve these high moments by symbols and ceremonies.

And in the course of history certain symbols have been

elevated to the status of what we call sacraments. A sacrament is "an outward and visible sign of an inward and spiritual grace." But I believe I speak for all groups when I say that the Lord's Supper is so central to the whole sacramental system that when the layman hears the term "sacrament" he almost instinctively thinks of the Last Supper.

As the Scripture says, our Lord knew what was in man. He knew that man is not a cold-blooded, matter-of-fact being who lives by logic and pure reason. Jesus knew that ideas to be remembered must be picturesque and duties to be gripping must be dipped in emotion. Hence Jesus did not merely say that God is our Father. He pictured God the Father in the unforgettable parable of the prodigal son. Jesus did not merely teach that men are meant to be brothers and neighbors. He dramatized what brotherly and neighborly love is in the story of the good Samaritan. And when he came to die, Jesus did not merely say, "I am with you always, even unto the end of the world." He did say that. But he did more. He spent the last night of his earthly life celebrating with his disciples a historic festival of his nation. And he transformed that commemoration of the Jewish Passover into a memorial of his own passion which has carried the conviction of his continuing presence even unto the end of the world.

The record as given by Luke is: "And when the hour was come he sat down, and the twelve apostles with him. And he said unto them, With desire I have desired to eat this passover with you before I suffer: For I say unto you, I will not any more eat thereof, until it be fulfilled in the kingdom of God. And he took the cup, and gave thanks."

Let us think on that scene until its portent sinks into our hearts. "And he took the cup and gave thanks." What does that cup symbolize?

At first it seemed the symbol of necessary sorrow. When we turn back to the Old Testament, we find some striking and symbolic references to the cup. In the seventy-fifth psalm the psalmist is picturing God as a judge, and he says: "In the hand of the Lord there is a cup, and the wine is red." In the fifty-first chapter of Isaiah the prophet cries to Jerusalem: "Awake, awake, stand up, O Jerusalem, which hast drunk at the hand of the Lord the cup of his fury." And Jeremiah, speaking of the Edomites who wished an easy escape from hardships, says: "Behold, they whose judgment was not to drink of the cup have assuredly drunken." In these references the cup symbolizes that which God pours out for man to drink, this meed of sufferings, which, as we say in colloquial language, we have to swallow. Of course the cup of life which we have to drink contains blessings as well as sufferings, as witness the twenty-third psalm, "My cup runneth over. Surely goodness and mercy shall follow me all the days of my life." But since the prophets felt called to rebuke and reform, the symbolism of the cup in their hands took the somber meaning.

It was in the sense of the cup as the bitter portion of life's necessary hardships that Christ used the word when he knelt in Gethsemane and prayed, "O my Father, if it be possible, let this cup pass from me." It was in this same sense that Jesus replied to the sons of Zebedee when their mother asked that they might have first places when he came into his Kingdom. He said to them, "Are ye able to drink of the cup that I shall drink of?" That is, in plain blunt language, "Can you stand up and take the bitter medicine which I shall have to swallow?"

Surely the wine was blood red in the cup of suffering which our Lord drank. Yet he drank it—drank it without flinching, saying in Gethsemane, "Father, if thou be willing, remove this cup from me: nevertheless not my will, but thine, be done." He drank it with the brave smile of a winning sportsman, saying to his comrades, "Be of good cheer; I have overcome the world." He drank it without bitterness toward those who inflicted it, praying from the cross, "Father, forgive them; for they know not what they do."

And now look at that cup again. Because he drank it as he did, that cup of suffering was transformed in our Lord's hands into the cup of grace. We all have to drink some bitterness from life's cup. The person who cannot stand up to life and swallow the bitter with the sweet is something less than a man. But the cup which Christ drank contained more than this necessary suffering common to all men. So far as outward compulsion was concerned, Christ could have escaped the cross. He said, "No man taketh [my life] from me, but I lay it down of myself." He went to the cross only through the compulsion of love. He had come into the world to save sinners. He had come to reveal the love of his heavenly Father. And to fulfill that mission he loved even to the end. He gave the last full measure of devotion. He surrendered his life not merely as a patriot dies for his own country, not merely as a martyr dies for a cause, but as a Saviour dying to redeem all men of every tongue and race and nation. Thus Christ revealed the grace of God.

And the divine grace thus revealed melts and moves the heart of man. Isaac Watts voiced our response in his familiar hymn:

> See, from His head, His hands, His feet,
> Sorrow and love flow mingled down:

Did e'er such love and sorrow meet,
    Or thorns compose so rich a crown?

Were the whole realm of nature mine,
    That were an offering far too small;
Love so amazing, so divine,
    Demands my soul, my life, my all.

The cup we may have to drink may have some bitterness
in it. But by the grace of God we can take it if we can lift
our eyes from the grim necessities of these times to the
overflowing love of him who died for us.

And now let us go on with the record. Jesus handed the
cup to his disciples, saying, "I will not drink of the fruit of
the vine, until the kingdom of God shall come," or as
Matthew puts it, "until that day when I drink it new with
you in my Father's kingdom." In Christ's hand the cup
becomes not only the cup of suffering and of grace but also
the cup of hope. Jesus turned the thoughts of his disciples
from the foggy darkness of that fateful last night to the
dawn of a new day.

When hope shines through a night like that, there must
be a powerful light behind it. To stand on the eve of one's
own death and talk calmly and confidently about the future
is a test of faith and hope which only the strongest can
stand. Here is vivid demonstration that "tribulation worketh
patience; patience, experience; and experience, hope."

The most convincing feature of Christian hope is that it
grows best in the soil of suffering and struggle. The sweetest
spirits I know are those whose lives have been full of bitter
experiences, while the sourest old cynics of my acquaintance
are those who on the surface have had what seemed a sweet
time of it most of their lives. It is a fact of history that the

literature of hope has come out of the environment of burdens and crosses, while the literature of pessimism has been written in the circles of comfort and prosperity. Recall the parlor cynics and penthouse pessimists back in the booming days of the 1920's. Recently in my parish we heard a series of speakers in our own school of missions. One was a Negro bishop, a man of most sensitive and refined nature, who has tasted the bitter cup which his race has had to drink; but he was not bitter or despairing. Another was a doctor recently returned from China, with that nation's sufferings and tensions fresh in her mind. But she still believes in the greatness of China's future and is going back at the earliest opportunity. Another was a former missionary to Japan. He was a realist about Japan who saw the perils long before Pearl Harbor; yet he looks forward confidently to future work in that land where a Christian remnant is the hope of redemption and reconciliation. After hearing these various speakers one thoughtful listener said, "Isn't it heartening to hear the Christian answer to our confused world?"

Ah, yes, the Christian answer to our confused world. That is what we need to hear, for it is the answer of hope. And as Paul said, "we are saved by hope." But someone will say, "We are saved by grace, not by hope." Well, both are necessary. In the work of salvation, grace is the attitude of God; hope is the response of man. And God's grace is the ground of man's hope. That is why I for one still have confidence that out of the sufferings of this present time will come a deeper sympathy; out of the collapses of human cleverness will come a greater dependence on divine help; out of the common sacrifices of nations will come a wider spirit of unity. If Robert Louis Stevenson with his pain-wracked body could lie down "with the half of a broken hope for a pillow at night" and still believe

> That somehow the right is the right
> And the smooth shall bloom from the rough,[1]

who am I to lose hope? If Christ could go to his cross holding out the promise of drinking the cup anew in God's kingdom, then I can hope too. And I will hope.

I am trying to lift up in thought the cup which our Lord drank. I have called it the "Lord's countersign." In the old days of warfare when an unrecognized person approached camp, the sentinel halted him with the command to approach and give the countersign. In this day of struggle can we approach the Lord's company and give the countersign? Can we stand with him and drink the cup of suffering, of grace, of hope? When the sons of Zebedee were challenged by our Lord with the question, "Are ye able to drink of the cup that I shall drink of?" they answered, "We are able." At the time they made the answer they were far from able. But by God's grace they became so. One of them, James, died for his Lord; the other, John, lived a long, useful, sacrificial life for his Lord. They passed and gave the countersign. They entered into the company of their Lord.

Are we able to drink the cup? Not in our own strength. But by God's grace let us try it together.

---

[1] "If This Were Faith" from *The Complete Poems of Robert Louis Stevenson*, copyright 1923 by Charles Scribner's Sons. Used by permission.

A Sacrament of Strength

JAMES M. LICHLITER

In a recent biography of General Sherman the author tells of an incident which occurred during the battle of Shiloh. The Confederate Army under General Albert Sidney Johnston had pushed the Union troops back almost into the river. In the midst of the carnage a teamster was struggling with a gun carriage which had become mired in the river bank. He was floundering about in the mud with his shoulder down against the wheel when a preacher came up to him and asked him in a ghostly voice, "Do you know who died on a cross?" Without looking up, and still straining against the wheel, the teamster shouted back, "Don't ask me any riddles. I'm stuck in the mud!"

That's a good story to begin with when we're tackling a matter like the Holy Communion. It's so frightfully easy to get lost in riddles. This service has the beauty of something rare and very old, and one can almost smell the dust of the ages upon it. The words themselves suggest the mystery of great antiquity. They have a quaint, archaic ring. Propitiation, oblation, satisfaction, sacrifice, divine mystery, advocate, mediator, the body and the blood, the Lamb of God—here's a stream of vague phrases, ancient concepts, thought forms which were once congenial but are now anachronistic and, as Edwin E. Aubrey puts it, "move like men in doublets through a modern factory." What does it all mean? What is there in it for average folks who are facing problems and tensions of everyday life in these times? Some of us are carrying burdens beyond our immediate resources—the loneliness of bereavement, the emptiness of a broken home. Others are fighting fear—that dumb, taut feeling in the throat day and night. Still others are bogged down where the going is hardest and everything is a problem and it takes a maximum of effort to achieve a minimum result. Then add to that the wear and tear of winter illnesses, uncertainty in business, troubles in home management, emotional stresses set up by war moves and broadcasts, and the countless irritations that a day of revolutionary change brings. Where does the Holy Communion fit into the picture? "Don't ask me any riddles. I'm stuck in the mud!"

Let us begin at the beginning. It was over nineteen hundred years ago. Jesus and his friends sat in the upper room of John Mark's house in Jerusalem having their last meal together. And when it was over, Jesus rose and took a piece of unleavened bread, broke it, and gave it to them with the words, "Take, eat; this is my body." Then he reached for the cup; and after he had given thanks, he gave it to them, saying, "This is my blood of the new testament, which is shed for many." He spoke, of course, in the vivid metaphor of the East. Dr. Fosdick tells of a native-born Syrian who when receiving a friend into his home says with extravagant hospitality, "This house is yours; you can burn it if you wish. My children also are at your disposal; I would sacrifice them all for your pleasure." "That's how your Oriental speaks. That language is graphic, suggestive, symbolic; not literal. And for men to take these words of Jesus in their literal sense is like insisting that the sun actually rises and sets because we use such terms. The disciples that night knew what he meant. He was leaving behind with them a memorial of himself. The broken bread was a little token that would symbolize for all time the essential character of his life and teaching, and so keep him ever in the minds of men. He had written no books, had founded no church, had not even bothered to appoint a successor. But in this simple ceremony he summed up concretely what he stood for, and trusted that to work when he was gone. A memorial, symbolizing sacrificial love. "This do in remembrance of me."

Then tragic things happened. Christianity moved out into a world full of cults, where the idea of communion meant partaking of deity. And soon this simple ritual was overlaid with superstition, and this memorial became magic. In the third century one heard that typical ecclesiastic, Cyprian, reporting that a woman who surreptitiously took the elements "received not food but a sword" and got "convulsions," and that a guilty man once found the bread turned to cinders. In the Middle Ages they rang bells before the consecration so that those in the fields could come running to behold the miracle when the bread and wine were changed into the body and blood of Christ.

Not only that. The Lord's Supper became as well a signal for strife and gainsaying among Christians, so that even today those from the various churches can work together, play together, sing and worship together, but they cannot take Communion together. Why? Because of a blasphemous tradition. There are men in every church who have the effrontery to believe that their particular way of doing things is patented in heaven and that Communion is invalid unless performed by their officials. As though anyone could monopolize the grace of God and by his particular church machinery control his power! If that isn't blasphemy, what is? Curiously enough, such abuses set in early. The Gospel of John, written at the end of the first century, doesn't record the institution of the sacrament; the scholars feel it was a deliberate omission. Already the Lord's Supper was being spoiled by magic and materialism. And so in protest the evangelist substituted the story of Christ washing the disciples' feet. The main thing in Christianity, says John, is love. "The servant is not greater than his lord."

So underscore this point first of all: the Holy Communion is symbolic through and through. It is a concrete and dramatic way of remembering Christ: the sort of man he was, how he lived and died, the one big thing he stood for. But now take the next step. Symbols, like charges of electricity, are dynamic things; and they help to energize a man's whole spiritual life. A great religious interpreter of our day said that he kissed his child because he loved her and that he kissed her in order to love her more. He was a realist. Love has its tangible symbols; and when one neglects them, the sentiment itself is apt to die. For most of us the word "home" is charged with deep emotion; but that emotion, mind you, is conjoined with concrete things: a particular house somewhere in a particular neighborhood, kitchen table, certain pictures, familiar chairs, the old piano, and walls that have soaked up memories and tears and laughter. Take away this material setting and let folks shift restlessly from one furnished apartment to another, and the family bond is weakened. Then, too, every nation, like the church, has its cultus: flags, anthems, and emblems; days of solemn commemoration; statues, monuments, and tombs of great men—all calculated to inspire and sustain the feeling of loyalty. More than we realize, perhaps, life is compelled by its symbols. Ideas, values, loyalties, and sentiments are all bound up with and depend upon concrete associations. In this world spiritual things do not exist in the abstract. We live, as Hegel observed, by "materialized thinking."

The point is that symbols are important because they are loaded with suggestive power. Here is a piece of silk with stars sewed on it, waving in the wind. The material itself is not precious—like radium for instance. Yet we treat it respectfully, and the sight of it stirs up a passion we would die for. Why? Because over the years we have invested in the flag our love of home and liberty, our democratic faith, our gratitude for the benefits anud privileges we have received, our missionary zeal that would extend and perfect this way of life. The flag means all these things and more to us: represents them, is the focal center, the magnetic core around which all our patriotic feelings gravitate.

That is how symbolism works. It is like the charging of a battery, says Huxley. The energy stored up in it flows back again.

So in this matter of the sacrament. The bread and the wine are common material substances. Yet they are charged with emotional power because of what Christ means to us. The late G. H. Studdert-Kennedy made it very clear: "I might pluck a rosebud off a tree," said he, "and it would be a rosebud and no more. The one I love best in all the world might pluck a rosebud off a tree and give it to me, and it would be a rosebud and a great deal more. The substance would be changed because she gave it to me." What the flag is to the patriot, the sacrament is to the Christian: a symbol of his ultimate allegiance, of all that is highest and holiest in human life, and so by reason of that fact a symbol loaded with suggestive power.

Here is no medieval magic. It's a far cry from this to the old theory that the bread and the wine are changed by sacerdotal power into the body and blood of Christ and that we are mysteriously strengthened by eating an invisible divine substance. Communion is not like swallowing a pill to get rid of a headache. Instead, it is an act of friendship. What the theologians call the grace of God and what you and I call inspiration and moral growth can get into a man only one way: through the mind and the affections. As the dean of Episcopal preachers, Phillips Brooks, once said: "There is no strength that is communicable except in character. It is the moral qualities of Christ's nature that are to enter into us and be ours—*because we are his.*" The process at bottom is quite simple. Communion helps a man because as a ritual it makes him think of Christ. It is an act of loyalty that deepens loyalty and through association brings uplifting forces into play. A strong friend gives his strength to those who love him. It was said of Robert E. Lee that he so immersed himself in the study of George Washington that one of his secrets was a grip on the character of Washington as a model, a hope, and a light. John Middleton Murry tells of one of his schoolteachers whose face betrayed such moral beauty that whenever the boys marched by him they would instinctively pull themselves together. There was a world of difference between Saul of Tarsus and Paul the Apostle, but it did not come about by accident. He had changed his friends. "I live; yet not I, but Christ liveth in me." That's how it works. I began by calling this a service of remembrance. It is more than that. It is a sacrament of strength. "I am the bread of life," said Jesus; "he that cometh to me shall never hunger; and he that believeth on me shall never thirst."

Leslie Weatherhead tells of a friend who attended a Roman Catholic mass, during which in the sermon the priest argued for the literal presence of Christ's body in the consecrated wafer on the altar, or what is technically called the doctrine of transubstantiation. After the service he met one of the worshipers and asked him if he believed all that the priest had said. The worshiper, an old man, answered this way: "When I come to mass, sir, I cannot follow what they do up at the altar. I just kneel down and think about Jesus. I think of that last week with his friends and the last supper; how he knelt in agony at Gethsemane; how they arrested him and all night tortured him; and how he died. . . . I get very near to Jesus then, sir, and when I go home I feel that he comes with me." That is all. That is enough!

The Art of Remembering

HENRY HITT CRANE

Man is distinguished from all other living beings by one fact we seldom consider. He is the only animal who builds tombs. He has been defined as the animal who laughs, or who uses tools, or who makes fire, or who thinks, or who speaks; but certainly he is the only animal that erects sepulchers.

He builds houses; so do muskrats and birds. He organizes into co-operative society; so do bees. He forms armies, under captains and generals; so do ants, which also have hospitals for the sick and schools for the young. There are insects and other lower forms of animal creatures that weave and spin, set traps, and hunt game. But no earth denizen save man buries its dead and puts up a tombstone or a marker. Almost all other human instincts, but not this, can be traced back to the brute. Only human beings have the instinct to preserve the remembrance of themselves upon the earth. Hence they build tombstones.

Man has always wanted to be remembered. As far back as the race is found there are markers of graves dumbly seeking to keep alive a faded fact. The remains of tombs are more ancient than the remains of dwelling places. Cities of the dead, in archeology, antedate cities for the living. What will men not do to keep from being forgotten! We build mausoleums, erect monuments, write books, give gifts, endow colleges, strive to achieve greatness this way and that, daring the perilous and the monotonous, struggling, aspiring, toiling—just to be remembered.

There is no doubt but that it is sweet to be remembered and bitter to be forgotten. It is a hard thing to feel at the close of a long life that one has been playing, as children do by the sounding sea, writing all day upon the sands only to watch the coming waves wash it all out before our eyes; or, as boys do in winter, writing upon the snow only to see it covered by other snow or melted from sight by the sun or rain; to pile all one's goods within stone walls and wake in the morning and find ashes; to stake one's life upon an office and lose it and shrink into obscurity; to lie down at night and die with the ears filled by the sounding and the eyes dazzled by the glistening of the coming tide that shall wipe all our lifework from the light and sight of day. And the higher a man's thoughts, the broader his sympathies, the deeper his love for his fellow men, the more awful the thought that he may be forgotten.

If mortal man feels so, if the average human being thus recoils from the fact of forgetfulness, how, indeed, must the Master of men have felt? He knew what was in man. He therefore knew how great the tendency to forget, particularly when the human mind is unaided by constant reminders of a material nature, something one can handle and see. He likewise knew that except as men remembered him and taught others of him the hope of Christianity would perish from the earth.

Did it ever strike you as a bit strange that, in marked contrast to most all great rulers of men, Jesus never built himself a monument of stone? We have no record that he ever wrote a word, except perhaps when he wrote on the sands. Yet Christ yearned to be remembered. He felt and uttered, as no other has done, the heart's deep, true protest against being forgotten. So he left us a marvelous memorial —marvelous in its simplicity, significance, and success.

As he sat in the upper room with his loved ones that darkening Thursday night and made his last requests, he did not ask that they build him a towering tomb—that could be visited but seldom. He avoided all mention of the ordinary memorials. He took the bread and the wine and said, "Eat . . . , drink . . . , this do in remembrance of me." Each time that ye shall eat and drink, think of me. The marble monument shall crumble and decay, the hand of the vandal shall break it, the foot of the destroyer shall trample it to dust; but so long as seedtime and harvest shall bring bread to the land, so long as the waters shall cover the face of the earth, so long shall Christ have a new monument. When bread fails, life goes out. Until bread fails, Christ's memorial is sure.

"This do in remembrance of me." In establishing this simple memorial service Christ ministered to one of the deepest needs of human life: the need of remembering. Have you ever thought what life would be without memory? What gravitation is to matter, memory is to mind; without the former buildings would vanish like mist, and the solid earth would disappear like a cloud; without the latter mind would be a mockery and worse. Memory is to thoughts what the silken cord is to the beads, holding them in place. The blood is the life of the body, and memory is the life of the soul; and when memory becomes sluggish, the powers are paralyzed. "This do in remembrance"—that you might keep alive and vital and strong the God-life of your soul.

You wonder, perhaps, that he did not say, "Trust me, have faith in me, hope for me, love me," at this last supper. You cannot trust, believe, hope, love, what memory fails to represent to you. And when you remember him, you cannot fail to trust, believe, hope, and love. Christ bids us remember him, well knowing that when his hand presses the keyboard of memory, the music of faith, hope, and love shall fill the soul.

"This do in remembrance of me." He touched another great fact in human life when he made this royal request. Men become like the thoughts they harbor, like the memories they cherish. Whatever a man's mental life is, is bound to affect his transactional life. It is the veriest truth that "as [a man] thinketh in his heart, so is he." As we entertain bad thoughts, our own character becomes bad, cheap, and common. As we hold high and holy memories, our lives are made strong and beautiful and great. To remember him, to cherish the thought of him, is to harbor heaven in your heart. It is not what the swift sweep of thought bears over the mind that enriches or impoverishes, but the deposit that memory holds; and when Christ would bless the world, he bade it think of, aye, remember him, for what we remember really blesses, as what we save and not what we earn enriches. He knew what nineteen hundred years have taught and experience has tested, that he, the personal Christ, was best worthy of remembrance, and they who remember him most become most like him, and therefore best.

"This Do in Remembrance of Me"

CLARENCE E. MACARTNEY

Today, after more than sixty-five generations have come and gone, we do this in remembrance of Christ!

Many great and beautiful things have been done in remembrance. Some of the noblest buildings ever erected by the hands of man have been memorials to those who died. Great hospitals, universities, and churches have been reared in remembrance of those who have lived and died. But here we have the greatest monument to memory. In the upper chamber of a home in Jerusalem a man is speaking to twelve poor men. This night he will be betrayed by one of them into the hands of his enemies, and tomorrow he will die as a malefactor on the cursed tree. Before their assembly breaks up, he consecrates the ordinary Jewish supper of bread and wine, and asks them to repeat that feast in memory of him when he is gone. Nineteen centuries have passed since then, and yet never a week has passed in all those years that his followers have not remembered him in the Lord's Supper.

The Bible makes great use of the faculty of memory. Again and again in the Old Testament, God says to the people of Israel, "Remember." "Remember that thou wast a bondsman in Egypt." "Remember the days of old." "Remember all the way which the Lord thy God hath led thee." "Remember, and do all my commandments." "Remember now thy Creator in the days of thy youth." "Remember the Sabbath day, to keep it holy." Jesus makes use of one of man's greatest and noblest and tenderest faculties, memory, to build his Church and bind his disciples to him. He establishes a Supper by which his people in all future ages will remember him.

When Ulysses, on his memorable journey through the islands and lands of the Mediterranean on his way home to Ithaca after the Trojan War, was about to leave the enchanted isle where Calypso lived, she came down to the beach as the ships were putting off and said to him, "Say good-by to me, but not to the thought of me." In this Supper, Christ secured that his friends would not say good-by to the thought of him but would remember him from age to age. The Lord's Supper sums up all the mystery of Christ and all the great doctrines of our Christian faith. All the tenderness and pathos and hope of Christ and his redemption speak to us at this table as we hear him say, "This do in remembrance of me."

We remember the life of Jesus. On the Wisconsin monument to the memory of her young men who perished in the terrible stockade at Andersonville, Georgia, during the Civil War are inscribed two lines from a stanza of Thomas Campbell's poem "Hallowed Ground":

> And is he dead, whose glorious mind
> > Lifts thine on high?
> To live in hearts we leave behind
> > Is not to die.

The remembrance of Christ and his glorious mind and life lifts our own souls on high. One of those who sat that night at the table with Jesus afterward wrote of him that he "[left] us an example that we should follow in his steps." And what a beautiful example it is that he left unto us! That very night he left a moving example of his humility, when, girding himself with a towel, he, to whom all dominion hath been given, took a basin and washed the disciples' feet and told them that in the same spirit of humility and ministry they should deal with one another. "If I then, your Lord and Master, have washed your feet; ye also ought to wash one another's feet. For I have given you an example, that ye should do as I have done to you." Humility was our Lord's favorite virtue, and for those who work and worship together in the Christian Church it is the virtue for which they ought to strive above all others.

When we remember the life of Jesus, we remember his prayerfulness, how that night when he took bread, he gave thanks, and how afterward in his sublime prayer he prayed for his disciples that they might be kept from the evil that is in the world, and that they might be one in Christian faith and love. We remember, too, how Jesus resisted temptation and said to the devil when he tempted him, "Get thee behind me!" That was something about Jesus that Peter was going to forget that very night. If he had remembered it, he might not have fallen.

When we remember the life of Jesus, we remember his compassion and sympathy, his forgiving spirit, and how he prayed for those who crucified him, "Father, forgive them; for they know not what they do." And we remember that beautiful and tender affection and loyalty which he showed to those men with whom he ate this Supper. The one who leaned upon his breast, and perhaps knew his heart better than any other, said, "Having loved his own which were in the world, he loved them to the end."

Thus all the strength and beauty of the life of Jesus rises before us when we sit at his table and hear him say, "This do in remembrance of me." What about you and me since the last Communion? How many times have you forgotten him? Remember, then, the life of Jesus, and walk in his steps.

We remember the death of Jesus. In Paul's account of the Lord's Supper, which is the earliest account we have, he adds a word of his own to that sentence of Jesus, "This do in remembrance of me." This is what Paul adds: "For as often as ye eat this bread, and drink this cup, ye do show the Lord's death till he come." It is plain that Jesus laid solemn emphasis upon his death. That is why the Gospels give such extraordinary space to it in their brief biographies of Jesus. This is in contrast with all other biographies, and all other men. We celebrate the birth of the world's great men but not their death. But what we celebrate most of all in the history of Jesus, and what he asked us to celebrate most of all, is his death. By his death he asks to be remembered. He came into the world by the great miracle of the Incarnation, when the angels sang, and shepherds and Wise Men came in adoration to his cradle. When he was baptized, the heavens were opened, and a voice spake saying, "This is my beloved Son." When he conquered temptation and Satan in the desert, the angels came and ministered to him. When he was transfigured on the mount, Moses and Elijah appeared and spake with him about his coming death on the cross, and again the voice spake from heaven, saying, "This is my beloved Son, in whom I am well pleased." After his death he rose again from the dead and appeared to his disciples, and after forty days he was taken up into heaven, and a cloud received him out of their sight. But it was not by his incarnation, or his baptism, or his temptation, or his transfiguration, or his resurrection, or his ascension, and not by any great miracle which he wrought, or any sermon which he preached, but by his death that Jesus asked to be remembered.

Why this pre-eminence to his death? Because of what his death meant. And what it means he explained to the disciples just before he said to them, "This do in remembrance of me." He said that as he broke the bread which was to feed their bodies, so his body was broken for their spiritual nourishment; and as he poured out the wine for their refreshment, so his blood was shed for the remission of sins. By this offering of himself on the cross, and by his death, he saves us.

When, then, in this Supper we remember the death of Jesus, we remember that we are all sinners and that it is only his death for us on the cross that can take away the stain and sting and penalty of our sin. When we remember his death, we cast all our trust upon him for our salvation. When we remember his death, we remember the worth of our souls. At times we realize how unworthy we are, how unworthy even of what men do for us, and still more, how unworthy of what God has done for us. And yet when we remember that Christ died for us, we know the infinite value of our soul because he paid so great a price to redeem our soul. When we remember the death of Christ, it strengthens us against temptation, for the memory of sin forgiven is like an angel with a drawn sword to keep us back from the way of evil and of death.

We remember that Christ will come again. In Paul's comment on the words of Jesus he says, "As often as ye do eat this bread, and drink this cup, ye do show the Lord's death till he come." Jesus was going on the morrow to a shameful, cursed death on the cross; and yet he had said that he would come again. If death had been the end, then the death of Jesus would never have been celebrated. But now we celebrate and show his death as a pledge of our faith that he will come again.

This was a death that ended death, and that leads to victory. By his death and resurrection Christ destroyed him who had the empire of death, that is, Satan. Today we may think there are very few signs of that victory. We behold a church divided, a world in turmoil and darkness, dreading a terrible Amageddon. It may look more like the victory of Satan than the victory of God. Yet whenever we celebrate this feast and show the death of Christ, we show the victory of his kingdom. The dying thief said to Jesus, "Remember me when thou comest into thy kingdom." If even a dying thief could see a conqueror in that thorn-crowned sufferer at his side, surely we can. As we celebrate the death of Jesus, we see here the light of the everlasting day. We hear the strains of triumphant music. "Steals on our ear the distant triumph song." We hear him who cried on the cross, "It is finished!" cry at length from the throne of a redeemed universe, "It is finished! The kingdoms of this world are become the kingdoms of our Lord and of his Christ, and he shall reign forever and ever." We hear him say to all of us today, "Be of good cheer; I have overcome the world."

All this great work of Christ in his life, in his death, in his coming again, is for you, for me. That is the way to take it—He died for me. He loved me and gave himself for me. These things we should remember when we partake of the Holy Communion.

The Master's Memorial

CLYDE V. HICKERSON

Is there anything in our Christian worship more
beautiful and suggestive than the Last Supper? It is a continuing challenge to every Christian to respond to the
matchless devotion of Christ with a purer devotion of his
own. It is the abiding witness of the love and compassion
of the Saviour for all mankind. If Horace, the poet, could
exultantly say of the songs he wrote, "I have reared a monument more enduring than bronze," then with far deeper
meaning and wider application can these words be applied to
the memorial Supper instituted by Christ.

The observance of and emphasis upon this act of worship
differs in various churches and denominational groups. Amid
these differences, however, there are some beliefs and prac-
tices held in common by Christians throughout the world.
For one thing the Communion is a feast of memory. Luke
reports that Jesus said on the night of the betrayal in the
upper room, "This do in remembrance of me," and Paul in
his account of the Lord's Supper in the eleventh chapter
of First Corinthians repeats this statement.

Christians need to be constantly reminded of the vital
matters of their faith and the implications of the gospel
for their lives. Throughout the Scriptures one sees the many
ways in which God seeks to keep certain significant events
in the minds of his people. The great feasts of the Hebrews
and their holy days were intended to remind the worshipers

of God's leadership and their dependence upon him. Thus the Passover reminded the Jews of the delivery from Egypt, and the Feast of the Tabernacles called to their attention the hardships of their forefathers in their march through the wilderness toward the land of promise. The book of Deuteronomy contains scores of warnings against forgetfulness and many exhortations to remember: "Beware lest thou forget Jehovah thy God"; "Thou shalt remember all the way which Jehovah thy God hath led thee" (8:12, 2 A.S.V.).

Simon Peter in his second epistle emphasizes the importance of a good memory on the part of Christians, "Wherefore I shall be ready always to put you in remembrance of these things, though ye know them, and are established in the truth which is with you. And I think it right, as long as I am in this tabernacle, to stir you up by putting you in remembrance" (1:12-13 A.S.V.). It is so easy to let vital things slip out of memory. We need often to bring these matters from the circumference of our minds to the central place in our thinking. Much effort must be given to reminding people of what they already know. While it is essential that we learn new truth, it is also necessary to recall that which we already believe. Dr. Samuel Johnson declared: "It is not sufficiently considered that men more frequently require to be reminded than informed." Living is like driving down a highway. There are road signs that indicate various things we should or should not do for safety's sake. It is not that we are ignorant of the rules of the road or that we do not know that trains go over the rails that we must cross, but we need at critical stages of the trip to be reminded of these things.

In *Pilgrim's Progress*, Samuel received the following answer to his question as to the place where his father fought Apollyon:

Your father had that battle with Apollyon at a place yonder before us, in a narrow passage, just beyond Forgetful Green. And indeed that place is the most dangerous place in all these parts. For if at any time pilgrims meet with any brunt, it is when they forget what favors they have received, and how unworthy they are of them.

The Lord's Supper was given to help us keep the sacrifice of our Saviour in mind. So in the upper room the night before the crucifixion Jesus took common bread and common wine, things found in the poorest of homes in Palestine, and exalted them into symbols of his life given a ransom for many. It did not seem likely in that hour that he would be remembered. In a little while he would be in his grave, having been executed as a criminal of the worst class. Surely everyone else thought the crucifixion would be the end of him. These last experiences of his earthly ministry, the climax of his redemptive work, being enshrined in the memorial Supper, have been kept fresh in the memory of his followers across nineteen centuries.

We are reminded, as we worship in the service of Communion, of the meaning of the cross for Christ and for his followers: "For as often as ye eat this bread, and drink this cup, ye proclaim the Lord's death till he come" (I Cor. 11:26 A.S.V.). Jesus said, "I am the good shepherd: the good shepherd layeth down his life for the sheep. . . . Therefore doth the Father love me, because I lay down my life, that I may take it again. No one taketh it away from me, but I lay it down of myself" (John 10:11, 17-18 A.S.V.). Leslie Weatherhead in his book *A Plain Man Looks at the Cross* sums up the meaning of Christ's death for him.

The words of Jesus about his suffering and death reveal that he willingly committed himself to some mighty task, costly to him beyond our imagining, but effecting for all men a deliverance beyond their own power to achieve, and that in doing so he knew himself to be utterly and completely one with God the Father.

> We may not know, we cannot tell,
> What pains he had to bear;
> But we believe it was for us
> He hung and suffered there.

It is at the cross that one realizes his unworthiness, feels the burden of guilt, and receives the assurance of forgiveness. "And he took a cup, and gave thanks, and gave to them, saying, Drink ye all of it; for this is my blood of the covenant, which is poured out for many unto remission of sins." (Matt. 26:27-28 A.S.V.)

Men and women since the beginning of Christianity have undergone a revolutionary change in their attitudes as they have thought upon the sufferings and death of Jesus Christ. More than a hundred years ago John Selwyn ministered to the cannibal Maoris of New Zealand. On one occasion he wrote:

I am in the midst of a sinful people, who have been accustomed to sin uncontrolled from their youth. If I speak to a native on murder, infanticide, cannibalism, and adultery, they laugh in my face, and tell me I may think these acts are bad, but they are very good for a native, and they cannot conceive any harm in them. But on the contrary when I tell them that these and other sins brought the Son of God, the great Creator of the universe, from his eternal glory to this world, to be incarnate and to be made a curse and to die—then they open their eyes and ears and mouths, and wish to hear more, and presently they acknowledge themselves sinners, and say they will leave off their sins.

Bunyan tells us in his immortal allegory that when Christian came up to the cross his burden fell from off his shoulders and rolled down into the sepulcher and he saw it no more.

Then was Christian glad and lightsome, and said with a merry heart, "He hath given me rest by his sorrow, and life by his Death." Then he stood still a while, to look and wonder; for it was very surprising to him that the sight of the cross should thus ease him of his burden. He looked, therefore, and looked again, even till the springs that were in his head sent the water down his cheeks."

Paul declares that Christ died for our sins, and Cowper the poet sings:

> Dear dying Lamb, thy precious blood
> Shall never lose its power,
> Till all the ransomed Church of God
> Be saved, to sin no more.

The Christian finds his faith strengthened as he tarries at the Lord's Table. He is reminded of Christ's continuing presence beyond Calvary. "But I say unto you, I shall not drink henceforth of this fruit of the vine, until that day when I drink it new with you in my Father's kingdom." (Matt. 26:29 A.S.V.) Christianity from its earliest days has united two elements, the historical and the mystical. Before the Ascension we have a ministry of outward contact, afterward a ministry of inward presence. Dr. Joseph Fort Newton said, "This dual nature of our religion has involved belief in certain facts about the life and work of Jesus, and at the same time it has meant an inward experience of union with God through him." There is a mystical element in the true observance of the memorial Supper, and the worshiper realizes anew the presence of his Lord.

> Shakespeare is dust, and will not come
> To question from his Avon tomb,
> And Socrates and Shelley keep
> An Attic and Italian sleep.
>
> . . . .
>
> They see not. But, O Christians, who
> Throng Holborn and Fifth Avenue,
> May you not meet, in spite of death,
> A traveler from Nazareth? [1]

There are many who as a result of partaking of the Communion find a deeper desire to be loyal to their Master and what he stood for.

William Wilberforce worked tirelessly for many years to free the slaves in the British Empire. After long agitation for emancipation a bill that evoked much argument was introduced in Parliament. One member had been bitterly opposed to the bill. When the vote was taken, to the surprise of all he voted in the affirmative. When one of his fellow members asked him why he had changed his stand so completely, he replied: "I spent last night with Wilberforce."

Yea, to spend one hour at the table of our Lord deepens our loyalty to him, strengthens our devotion to him, confirms our faith in him. James Montgomery long ago wrote the stanzas that express beautifully what devout Christians across the ages have felt as they have accepted the invitation of Christ to come to his table.

[1] "To and Fro About the City" from *Seeds of Time.* Copyright 1922 by John Drinkwater. Reprinted by permission of the Author's Estate.

The Master's Memorial

According to Thy gracious word,
 In meek humility,
This will I do, my dying Lord,
 I will remember Thee.

Thy body, broken for my sake,
 My bread from heaven shall be;
Thy testamental cup I take,
 And thus remember Thee.

Remember Thee, and all Thy pains,
 And all Thy love to me:
Yea, while a breath, a pulse remains
 Will I remember Thee.

And when these failing lips grow dumb,
 And mind and memory flee,
When Thou shalt in Thy Kingdom come,
 Jesus, remember me.

"Behold the Man"

F. GERALD ENSLEY

WHEN THROUGH THE SYMBOLS OF THE SACRAMENT WE recall the Crucifixion, we think about that dramatic scene where Jesus stands before Pilate. The time is the gray dawn of Good Friday. The Jews have haled the Master before the Roman governor. They want the Nazarene to be put to death; he has blasphemously claimed to be the king of the Jews. But Pilate in a brief examination sees that their case against him is flimsy. He finds no fault in the man and offers to release Jesus. But the crowd will not have it; they want his blood. Then Pilate has him whipped. The Roman soldiers twist thorns into a crown and put it on his head and in ridicule salute him as though he were a king and then slap him. When their raillery has at last grown tiresome, Pilate has the victim led forth. As they bring him out, Pilate cries, "Behold the man."

Think for a moment about those words of Pilate. Consider what Pilate meant by them, what they signified to the Jews, and finally their connotation for John, who reports the scene.

"Behold the man," said Pilate. He meant, "Look at the man; *he's harmless.*" The crowd had accused Jesus of wanting to be a king. But what a pitiable sight he is now as he stands before the governor. His garments are disheveled; his hair is matted with sweat and blood; his torso is a swollen pulp of welts. And Pilate says, in effect, "Look at this miserable creature. How can such a wretch as this be accused of treason? Why punish an unhappy fellow like this? Behold the man! Look him over. He's really harmless."

There are a great many modern people who think of Jesus as a harmless, inoffensive idealist. They regard the religion he founded as very lofty sentiment but far removed from reality. They acknowledge that there are people who get help from Jesus. His beliefs, if you can swallow them, have a soothing, therapeutic effect. But why should anyone get excited about him? His religion is beautiful idealism, and he was a beautiful character, but you must not take him seriously.

There are businessmen who talk that way. A minister friend of mine once read that passage from the Sermon on the Mount about not worrying because God feeds the ravens and clothes the lilies, even though they neither sow nor spin. A real estate man and a grocer happened to be sitting side by side in the same pew. The real estate man looked over at the grocer and smiled, as if he were saying, "Imagine being a lily in the real estate business." And the grocer smiled back, as if he were answering, "Yes, or a raven in the grocery business." By their looks they had thrown Jesus and his gospel right out in the aisle.

There are politicians who think the same about Christianity. Wayne B. Wheeler once went to Mark Hanna, the notorious political boss, and urged the election of a certain man, saying that the church folk of the state would support him. Hanna smiled and said, "Young man, your kind of people are all right in a prayer meeting, but they're not worth a hoot at a caucus." These Jesus-folk in the eyes of the politician are a harmless group.

There are professed Christian people who think of Jesus as tame and gentle. One of the greatest obstacles that ever stood in the way of my becoming a Christian was the way Christ was presented to me by my Sunday-school teachers. He was never presented as a hero or a manly man but always as something bordering on the sissy. "Behold the man," said Pilate. "He's harmless." And a host of other men since have affirmed the same.

But the test of validity is endurance. Pilate thought that when he had washed his hands of the Master he had finished him. It was like stepping on a worm to erase this miserable Nazarene. But the centuries have come and gone, and what has happened? Pilate is nothing more than an ugly memory. No one remembers his birth date; no one wants to. Yet we reckon time from the birth of the one whom Pilate thought he had finished. We sing and pray in the name of Jesus. Surely no one sings or prays in the name of Pilate. In Paul Muni's film of a few years ago, "The Life of Emile Zola," you may recall that the judge kept insisting that the Dreyfus case was closed—"This witness may not appear; this testimony may not be given; the affair of Dreyfus is a closed case." And as the court rose from its sitting with this repeated affirmation sounding like the knell of doom for both Dreyfus and Zola, the mural of the crucified Christ appeared over the judge's rostrum, and Zola's lawyer remarked that that, too, was once regarded as a closed case.

"Behold the man. How harmless he is!" Pilate thought he was passing the final judgment on his prisoner. But that case was not closed; that harmless man has outlived and outlasted the materialist who condemned him.

"Behold the man!" To the Jews those words meant, "Beware of the man. He's dangerous." Pilate thought of Jesus as harmless; the Jews thought of him as harmful. When Pilate brought Jesus out, they shouted with one voice, "Crucify him! Crucify him!" They hated him be-

cause at heart they were afraid of him. They knew that
the man before them stood for ideas which, if they got
loose in the world, would destroy them. With his universal
love for all men he was a threat to their sectarian exclusiveness. They hated him not because he was weak, but they
hated him because they knew that if he lived, eventually the
things they stood for would die. "Behold the man." To
those Jews in the courtyard that meant, "Beware of the
man. He's dangerous." And they wanted to crucify him.

Those Jews in that mob had much keener insight than
Pilate. They were not deceived by the fact that for the
moment the Master was weak through torture. They looked
beyond the broken body to the ideas and ideals that ani-
mated him. They saw what Pilate did not see. They saw
that the most powerful thing in all the world is an idea
embodied in a man.

On Commonwealth Avenue, Boston, there is an imposing
statue of William Lloyd Garrison, the famous abolitionist.
He wasn't much of a man, measured by materialistic
standards. He had never been to college; he was poor,
self-taught, and obscure. In 1831 he began to print a little
sheet called the *Liberator*. He started without a dollar of
capital or a single subscriber. He had no political influence,
few friends. All he had was a few ideas that happened to
be true and some paper and printer's ink. He was despised,
threatened, finally dragged by a mob through the streets
of Boston with a halter round his neck. Yet a later
generation erected a monument to his memory by popular
subscription. On one side of it are the words, "My country
is the world. My countrymen are mankind." That was his
idea. And on the other side one reads, "I am in earnest,
I will not equivocate, I will not excuse, I will not retreat
a single inch, and I will be heard." That was the spirit in

which he embodied his idea. Together they brought down the house which slavery built. There is nothing more powerful than an idea embodied in a man.

That's why the Jews were right. Jesus Christ is one of the most dangerous individuals who ever lived in our world. He's dangerous to anyone who wants to go in for easy living. As Mary Magdalene says in the book *By an Unknown Disciple*, "Jesus did not condemn me. I condemn myself. My punishment for having lived a dirty life is to see the beauty of a clean one, and he showed me that. It is enough."

This man Jesus is not only dangerous to easy virtue; he is dangerous to race prejudice. Believe me, you don't want Jesus around if you are going to treat men of other races as though they are inferior. Christ and prejudice cannot live together in the same heart.

This man Jesus is dangerous to dictators. Wherever the spirit of Jesus is, there is liberty. And wherever there is liberty, the dictators tumble. "Where is your carpenter now?" a Roman taunted one of the early church fathers after the crucifixion of Christ. "He's making a coffin for your emperor," replied the saint. And that is what the Carpenter has been doing ever since.

This man Jesus is the enemy of war. As long as the spirit of Christ is abroad in the world, the institution of war will have an enemy. James Russell Lowell used to say that there is enough dynamite in the Sermon on the Mount to blow the world to smithereens. And he was right. From the first century to this present hour Christianity has been a disturbing influence on the earth. "Behold the man." "Beware," said the Jews. "He's dangerous."

Well, thus far we've noted Pilate's view of Jesus, that he was harmless; and the Jews' attitude, that he was harmful. Let's consider now for a moment a third. On the fringe of the crowd the disciples were watching. Very likely John, the beloved disciple, was in the group. When Pilate said, "Behold the man," it meant to John, "the man, the man sent by God, the hope of the world." John had been reared in the great prophetic tradition of Israel. The prophets had foretold that one would come who would take upon himself the moral government of the world. He would not be a conqueror, but a man of sorrows and acquainted with grief. He would be wounded for men's transgressions, bruised for their iniquities. The chastisement of their peace would be upon him, and with his stripes would they be healed. As John looked upon that scene and reflected upon it afterward, it seemed to him that he saw the man the centuries had been promised and were looking for. "Behold the man —*the* man, the hope of the world."

John was right. That man whom Pilate pitied and the Jews feared *is* the hope of the world. The desire of every right-thinking person is for peace. We must break this awful cycle of war before it breaks us! Yet without the spirit of this man there is no peace. We crave domestic happiness, homes where people love each other supremely. Yet unless romantic love can be sustained by a sacrificial love that returns good for evil, suffers long and is kind, there can be no domestic tranquillity. No one would ever accuse George Bernard Shaw of being sentimental or of having prejudice toward Christianity. Yet these are his words:

I am ready to admit that after contemplating the world and human nature for nearly sixty years, I see no way out of the world's misery but the way which would have been found by Christ's will if he had undertaken the work of a modern practical statesman. . . . Though we crucified Christ on a stick, he somehow managed to get hold of the right end of it, and . . . if we were better men we might try his plan.

"Behold the man—the man, the hope of the world."

As we celebrate the sacrament, we should keep in mind that its meaning embraces the three dimensions of time. It is a memorial of the past, the recall of his earthly life with its atoning summit upon the cross. The bread and wine symbolize, too, his continuing presence which nourishes the devout believer. The Communion is also an account of that which is to come. Says Paul in one of the earliest accounts of the Lord's Supper, "As often as ye eat this bread, and drink this cup, ye do show the Lord's death till he come." The sacrament is the symbol of a hope—that in Jesus Christ we have the one for whom the centuries are looking and whose coming, in the flesh or the spirit, marks the consummation of all our moral striving.

Three Crosses Jesus Bore

HAROLD COOKE PHILLIPS

It is strange, this persistent appeal of the cross of Jesus. The list of the world's martyrs is an appalling one. But something there is about Jesus' crucifixion that has an appeal, a timelessness, a permanence, unmatched, yea, unapproached by any other martyrdom of the world's history. Here is something singular, different, unique.

Says George Tyrrell in his oft-quoted words: "Again and again I have been tempted to give up the struggle, but always the figure of that strange man hanging on his cross sends me back to my task again." Somehow we do not say that about any of the other heroic souls who have suffered and died for the truth. Might it be that "the difference between his cross and other crosses is the difference between him and other men"?

Moreover, though the cross was a symbol of disgrace, defeat, and death, in none of these attitudes do we find its real meaning. This is because Calvary cannot be separated from Joseph's garden. In our thinking Good Friday is always set against the background of Easter morning and Christ's suffering seen in the light of his triumph. This is why the cross is not a symbol of gloom but of glory.

I sometimes think that we are prone to overstress the purely physical aspects of Jesus' cross and so to miss the deeper spiritual overtones which give to Calvary its permanence and power in our lives. That is why we should think of three crosses Jesus bore. In truth Jesus bore the cross long before his body was nailed to it.

One of the crosses he bore might be called the "cross of constriction." "I have a baptism to be baptized with," he said, "and how am I straitened till it be accomplished." There are times when men would cleave the upper air, soar beneath the expanding spaces of the sky, but find their wings beating against the impinging bars of some cage. "How am I straitened." Have no doubt about it; that was one of the crosses Jesus bore.

Is not this indeed, as Bushnell once pointed out, the very meaning of the Incarnation? "The Word was made flesh" —God became man. The Infinite took upon himself the inevitable limitations of the finite. If we really believe that the one who submitted himself to all the limitations of human flesh, who knew hunger, weariness, and pain, bore in his deepest nature the impress of the Infinite, can we fail to see the shadow of the Cross in the very fact of the Incarnation? "How am I straitened"—the cross of constriction.

Think of the constriction that Jesus' nationality placed on him. He was born a Jew and lived his life within Jewish culture and tradition. It was a rich and meaningful tradition, but Jesus knew well that his life and his message could not be confined within such narrow limits. It was impossible for him to put the new wine within the old traditional wine-skins. His favorite designation of himself was not "Son of David" but "Son of man." He spoke of himself as being "the light of the world"—not of Judea. But during his earthly pilgrimage that universal yearning for all the sons of men had to be set in the narrow mold of national and racial exclusiveness. "How am I straitened."

Jesus was straitened by the inner compulsion which his mission imposed. A word frequently on his lips was "must."

"I must be about my Father's business." "I must work the works of him that sent me." Like the radio beam that guides a ship through the trackless air, so this inner compulsion kept him on his course. He never deviated. So he was constrained.

To a lesser extent many of today have to bear this cross. Often we are circumscribed by bodily limitations or afflictions, or by the forces of circumstance. Indeed, the very disciplines which the Christian faith imposes may seem to restrict. "The love of Christ constraineth us," said Paul. He spoke, moreover, of the "thorn in the flesh, the messenger of Satan" which, as he said, was sent "to buffet" him.

It is strange but true that it is through these very constraining experiences which seem to curtail, restrict, or circumscribe our life that life is liberated, enlarged, and enriched. We often think that the abundant life is achieved by kicking over the traces, jumping over the fences, and cavorting all over the lot. This is not so. The abundant life is rather achieved by these very disciplines which seemingly limit and narrow our field. It is no coincidence that this man Paul, who felt the constraining love of Christ, is the very man who wrote of "the glorious liberty of the children of God" and of "the breadth, and length, and depth, and height" of "the love of Christ, which passeth knowledge." "Strait is the gate, and narrow is the way, which leadeth unto life." The broad, easy road of effortless self-indulgence never takes one to any goal worth reaching. "The Son of man must." This inner compulsion became the source of his strength and his triumph. He must. We may.

There is another cross that Jesus bore, the cross of disappointment. It was of course impossible for him to escape that. This is always the cross of those who pioneer; and Jesus was called the "pioneer of faith." The shadow of this cross appeared at the very threshold of his ministry. In his temptation he was offered "the kingdoms of the world, and the glory of them." "All these things will I give thee." But while the world was offering him its kingdoms, he was saying to the world, "Seek ye first the kingdom of God, and his righteousness; and all these things shall be added unto you." Thus it became clear to Jesus that what his age offered him he could not accept, and that what he had to offer it did not want.

Consider the disappointment that must have grown out of the reaction of the public to his message. At first their response was encouraging; multitudes followed him. But as soon as they began to grasp the real nature of his message and to realize that it could not be fitted into the static and inadequate concepts of their traditional expectations, they began to leave him. This must have caused him deep regret, for he loved people. But he loved truth even more.

The public deserted him because he would not give them what they wanted. The politician can give the people what they want, but not the prophet. For the prophet has a bigger task to fulfill, namely, not that of giving the people what they want but what they need. His task is not that of pleasing them but of serving them. What did the people want? A king who would restore their nationalistic hopes and establish the kingdom of Israel. Jesus was interested in another kingdom, the frontierless kingdom of God, to which men would come from the East and from the West to sit down with Abraham, Isaac, and Jacob. What did the people want? Someone to fan the fires of racial and national pride. But Jesus came to kindle in men's hearts a compassion which transcended all particularisms of race or class. He came not to please people but to serve them. But people would rather be pleased than served. Hence he aroused their ire and antagonism, and they crucified him. Winifred Kirkland writes: "The three hours' agony of Jesus on his cross does not compare either in torture or in victory with the successive calvaries of scorn and disappointment that he had previously endured for thirty years." "O Jerusalem, Jerusalem, thou that killest the prophets, and stonest them which are sent unto thee, how often would I have gathered thy children together, . . . and ye would not!" "Lonely is a man of vision in a world that cannot see."

But keenly as Jesus must have felt the reaction of the public in general, no less must have been his disappointment with his intimate followers. They were none too alert. They learned but slowly. Even when he was going up to Jerusalem to die for a kingdom in which the greatest was to be the servant, two of them were quarreling among themselves as to who would occupy the most prominent seat. Three in Gethsemane were to fall asleep. One of the most trustworthy of them, since he was treasurer, was to betray him; his closest friend was to deny him thrice.

Who does not know from personal experience something about this cross? All know what it is to have hopes deferred, dreams that fade, cherished expectations that die, people that let us down. Indeed, he is very insensitive who does not feel today the weight of this cross arising from the very chaos of our age. We fought the First World War to make the world safe for democracy but instead set the stage for tyranny. We fought the second to overcome a tyrant and safeguard the four freedoms, and in doing so produced more tyrants than we destroyed. Moreover, from a Christian point of view how disappointing seems our lot. We believe in love, and the world is full of hate; in kindness, and we behold appalling cruelty; in brotherhood, and the world has flouted it; in peace, and there is a constant threat of war; in right, yet live in a world where all too often might makes right. "Where is the promise of his coming?" He would be an insensitive soul who does not bear the cross of disappointment. Let us thank God that Jesus bore that cross too.

Now when a man bears a cross like that, there are one or two courses he may take. As he sees his fondest hopes and choicest dreams—be they personal or social, private or public—perish and die, he may throw up the sponge and say, "What's the use?" He may sneer at life, his spirit bitter and cynical, completely disillusioned. Or perchance he may just drop out of sight, seek refuge, as many intellectuals do, in some ivory tower. But Jesus took neither of these courses because there was still another cross for him to bear. It was, of course, the cross of love. We call it Calvary.

"The greatest of these is love," said Paul. It is not surprising then that we have selected this cross as the epitome of Jesus' life. It includes and fulfills the others. This is our final and fullest thought of him: not the straitened man hemmed in by the impinging walls of circumstance, nor the disappointed man rebuffed by the dullness and hardness of men's hearts, but the man who loved and has given the highest and holiest expression of love the world has known, the love that is of God.

Maybe we too can pass from the cross of constriction and the cross of disappointment to the cross of love, in which we may find deathless victory and release from frustration.

On a visit to Russia before the days of the iron curtain Justice Wroe Nixon was walking back to his hotel one evening along the Moscow River. The sun was sinking. He wrote that its direct rays no longer reached the valley, nor the walls of the Kremlin, nor the palace of the czars, nor the flag of the Soviet Union that floated above it, but shone on the cross on the Church of the Assumption, the old church where the czars were crowned. That cross was still the highest point in the Kremlin.

As the sun sank below the horizon, its light lingered at the last on that cross, as if to suggest there was something in it that would be the last thing to die out in human life. Long after the czars had been forgotten, long after the Communists had gone on, and the wisdom of Marx had been gathered into the larger wisdom of the race—something in the Cross would still beacon to the human spirit. For it speaks not merely of time, but of eternity; not merely of power, but of love; not merely of man, but of God.

Just now it seems as though the light on that cross has gone out, as though the destructive forces of life so occupy the stage as to crowd all else off behind the wings. So too it seemed that day long ago. For then hate was pitted against forgiveness, and hate won; treachery against truth, and treachery won; cruelty against kindness, and cruelty won. In short, human stupidity and sin were pitted against divine love, and they won. But did they win? Had they actually, we could not sing today "In the Cross of Christ I Glory." Had they won, the green hill would long since have been lost in unrelieved darkness and despair. The victory of sin was as brief as it was brutal. Easter morning was to prove that the very means by which men sought to get rid of Christ became in God's good providence the open door through which the victorious Christ re-entered the life of men, to leave no more. Today the poet is asking:

> Speak, History! Who are life's victors?
> Unroll thy long annals and way,

Are they those whom the world called
   The victors, who won the success of a day?
The martyrs or Nero? . . .
   His judges or Socrates, Pilate or Christ?

And somehow deep in our hearts we know the answer.
As we take the Communion cup, we know his victory—
and ours.

The Meaning of the Cross

ANSLEY C. MOORE

Jesus is on trial before Pilate in the palace. Pilate
wants to release him, saying he can find no fault in Jesus.
But the mob outside is yelling, "Crucify him!" Pilate washes
his hands of the affair and says, "I am innocent
of the blood of this just person."

Our Lord, with calm dignity, allows himself to be turned
over to the soldiers to be crucified. These crude men of arms
mockingly bedeck him; they plait a crown of thorns and
put it upon his head, press those thorns until they prick the
tender flesh of his forehead as little streams of blood trickle
down. A traveler from Cyrene, Simon, is halted in his
journey and made to carry the cross. They go to Golgotha,
the "place of a skull," a promontory just outside the city
walls. The narrative in the twenty-seventh chapter of Matthew is so vivid that if you listen as you read, you can hear
the ring of the hammer as it pounds the nails into his hands
and feet. After nailing him there, they set the cross in a hole
in the ground, and they leave him with his physical suffering,
his mental anguish, and his broken heart to die.

We imagine that we can see through Jesus' eyes and
survey the groups which gather about the foot of the cross.
There are the soldiers. That must be a brutal lot. They little
dream that Jesus really is the Messiah, the Son of God. How
can they know; they are so stupid, so moribund. They have

crowned him with thorns. We have people today who, like the soldiers, crown Jesus with a crown of thorns.

Then there are "they that passed by." These wag their heads when they see Jesus; and they revile him, they rail at him, they curse him. As they shake their heads, they say in effect, "I told you so." "If thou be the Son of God, come down from the cross." The chief priests and scribes say, "He saved others; himself he cannot save." They despise him with a cordial hatred, and their slander is the bitterest of all.

It was because he saved others that himself he could not save. If he were willing to save himself, others would have been lost. Meekness here has its finest hour. The lowly Christ, showing the strength of meekness, bears not only the physical pain of crucifixion, not only the sins of these same ecclesiastical leaders, but their cruel mockery as well. Watching his patient demeanor from afar as he fails to strike back, we love him the more.

Turn now from the people beneath the cross to the person upon it. The sun is high overhead in the heavens when Jesus enters the six darkest hours of his earthly life. Someone has said that although it is near high noon, a deed is being performed on Golgotha from which even the sun itself must hide its face in shame. "From the sixth hour there was darkness over all the land." Jesus no longer sees the crowds below. Their mocking voices have been hushed as they felt the gloom of darkness at midday. The Saviour now, as the full weight of the sins of men descends upon him, forgets for a time those about him as he forgets the pain and the shame. The Redeemer of the world is again alone with God, and the sin of the world is on him. They offer him vinegar and gall to deaden the pain. The victim shifts his body to relieve the pain at one point only to increase it at others. Finally when the excruciating agony has deadened the body so that nerves no longer report the agony to the brain, Jesus feels a tragic loneliness sweep over his soul, a feeling that he has been forsaken by all, even his Father. The sense of forsakenness is a part of the evil that put him there, and forces from his otherwise silent lips, in the language he learned at his mother's knee, "My God, my God, why hast thou forsaken me?" There never was a time when God was nearer his Son. But there is in the heart of Jesus, under the circumstances, the feeling of forsakenness.

After three hours of darkness, and after what must have seemed a millennium to a soul as sensitive as his, Jesus gave up the struggle and died. It is unthinkable. His only crime had been that he loved men as they had never been loved before, but they were so unlike him that it was easier to lynch him than to be like him. So Jesus died. Bless him! He who once had cried out of a pastor's heart in a great upsurge of emotion, "O Jerusalem, Jerusalem, . . . how often would I have gathered thy children," died with that possibility cut off. Another has said, "The agony is over. The feeling of separation, of utter loneliness is gone, for the last word has been, 'Father, into Thy hands I commend my Spirit.' And as the spirit of the Son of Man returns to the Father's bosom, the gloom is gone, and the sun shines out again upon the earth."

We return for a moment to the foot of the cross, for there is one we have purposely passed by. "Now there stood by the cross of Jesus his mother, and his mother's sister, Mary the wife of Cleophas, and Mary Magdalene." And the disciple John is there. That is the little group that love Jesus and have now come to help him. Somehow I cannot forget Mary, mother of Jesus, on the crucifixion day. She stands looking up into the face of her son, her boy, if you please, for he is very young. She is dumbfounded, brokenhearted, completely crushed. Looking into his face, she thinks of the years of teaching him at her knee, the nights when she prayed for a reasonable outcome of this strange chain of events. She does not understand the blood, *her* blood, which is now upon the brow that a thousand nights she had fondled. I cannot forget the mother of Jesus as I look at those about his cross. Jesus does not forget her; in spite of all he remembers to commit her to his friend, John.

Such is the story of the greatest day in history. All the previous centuries of Grecian, Roman, and Jewish history point to the Atonement Day—day of at-one-ment between God and man—and all the centuries since look back upon it with wonder and awe, all of us knowing that we ourselves would not have been capable of anything so magnificent as the glorious madness of his self-sacrifice.

After trying to live with our Lord through these dark hours of suffering, after trying to feel in some small sense, at least, as he felt, and after trying sincerely to see through his eyes as he hung upon the cross, we let the curtain of two thousand years fall; and prayerfully we ask ourselves the question, Does this page from the life of Jesus mean anything more to me than a page from the life of Moses, or Washington, or Lincoln? What does the cross *actually* mean to me? Obviously that cannot be told in a word or a thousand words. It can only be suggested.

The cross means *light for our minds*. Life offers all of us discouragement on every hand. We look at nature and see her red tooth and claw. There is decay on all sides, disintegration, death. When we move up into the human realm, it is the same. Everywhere we look, we see sorrow, suffering, sin, and death. The best person we know dies of cancer. The grandest boy in the battalion is killed in battle.

The innocent child of the most loyal church member is run over by a car. Our minds are confused by these facts. We throw back our heads, beat our breasts, and cry to the universe for an explanation; but only the echo of our un-answered wail returns to us. Our restless minds send us off on inquiring quests, but each trail ends at long last in a cavern where there is only darkness. Is there no light for these minds of ours which hate the darkness as nature abhors a vacuum?

Someone has said that the answer to the riddle of the universe is God. The answer to the riddle of God is Christ. E. Stanley Jones adds, "The answer to the riddle of Christ is to be found in his sacrificial spirit culminating in his cross."

There is light here for our minds. At the cross of Christ we see the heart of the God who made this universe with all its discouraging features. To be sure, God is not the author of sin, but in his providence he permits the presence of evil things, else we cannot say that he is in control of his creation. At Calvary's cross we see the red heart of God laid bare, and it is revealed—marvel of marvels—that it is a heart of self-sacrifice. So the light is summed up in this: self-sacrifice is at the heart of this universe. All is not sorrow; all is not suffering; all is not death. Self-sacrifice, which is the culmination of the moral life; self-sacrifice, which calls forth from *all* mankind the distinctly moral response of reverence, is at the center of this whole creation. The cross of Christ shows this fact, and so we can say:

> In the cross of Christ I glory,
>   Towering o'er the wrecks of time;
> All the light of sacred story
>   Gathers round its head sublime.

The cross means *love for our hearts.* Jesus bridged the gap between the infinite and the finite. He brought God down to us and made us know God as a loving and a lovable God. Nothing so vividly reveals the love of God for us as Jesus' sacrificial death upon the cross. The cross somehow enables us to stand in the stream of God's love and to feel it enfold us. As we stand looking into the Saviour's eyes as he dies, we understand for the moment that his death is not for the masses of men only but for each of us personally. What a triumph to shout, Christ dies for *me!* The cross shows us the extent of that love, the height of it, the depth of it. It is intensely personal, this love of God revealed at the foot of the cross.

It is more than personal. It is transforming, redeeming. All of us wonder at times if we are just a dot on a cosmic speck of dust hurling through space at a terrific pace, without purpose, without meaning. Do we stand alone in this vast orbital system, surrounded by cold uninhabited heavenly bodies which do not come near again in a billion light years? The cross of Christ says otherwise. The warm love of God enters all our hearts as we, standing at the cross, take Christ by faith. We need never again feel lonely, for this love of God is ours forever. It is a *redeeming* love with power to forgive and to lift us, without violating our freedom, above our sinful natures. As long as the "old rugged cross" towers "o'er the wrecks of time," we can refresh our souls at the stream of God's mercy; and that portion of his love which we need will be supplied. We do not understand all that happened there that day, but we do know that Christ's cross has brought God's forgiving love to us.

I know not how that Calvary's cross
A world from sin could free;

> I only know its matchless love
> Has brought God's love to me.[1]

The cross means *life for our souls*. Robert Browning in his poem "De Gustibus" puts these words upon the lips of a character,

> Open my heart and you will see
> Graved inside of it, "Italy."

Life's experiences are not graven upon the heart in visible fashion, but if they were, there would be a cross imprinted indelibly upon my own. I see its outline every hour. I cling to it even as a drowning man clasps a straw. If it could be taken away from me, a part of my life would go. When the road is rocky and rough, and things go wrong, I look to this symbol which is emblazoned upon my heart. It is the symbol of new hope, of unrealized possibilities, of renewed life, of unlimited self-sacrifice. It is the symbol of the abundant life for me. So if I lose my grip upon Christ's cross, I lose my grip upon a way of life which is the grandest way, the only *real* way man knows. The cross means living *all my life* here and now.

But it means life in another sense for me. It means life everlasting. I do not know all that transpired in the secret councils of the Holy Trinity ere the Christ came. I know only that something happened outside the wicket gate that day which has changed my life permanently. Christ did me the signal honor of climbing down off his cross and walking straight into my heart! There he ascended the throne of my life. His love and his purpose for my life penetrated all the dark corners and gave a glow to the days. I then came into possession of the *quality* of life which I

[1] Copyright 1921 by Harry Webb Farrington. Used by permission.

know cannot end. It goes on and on and on. As I walk with Christ each day, as I merge my life with his each hour, I come to know that this is eternal life. I now have no doubt but that he and I—and all others of this wonderful way— will live forever. Using the medium of his Spirit, I shall step upon my own grave and on out into aeons of time. The cross brings that larger, richer life to me, life which knows no end.

> I know not how that Joseph's tomb
> Could solve death's mystery;
> I only know a living Christ,
> Our immortality.[2]

All this the cross means to me. And more.

The Perfect Sacrifice

CLARENCE TUCKER CRAIG

ONE OF THE MOST IMPORTANT ASPECTS OF THE SERVICE
of Holy Communion is that of sacrifice. And yet there are
many of us who fail to understand this familiar word. We
confuse so easily our hardships and misfortunes with sacrifices. Genuine sacrifice has nothing to do with little depriva-
tions or with petty discomforts. To sacrifice is to surrender
voluntarily what is good and precious on behalf of the
greater good.

The word had its origin in religion. Sacrifice began in the
belief that gods demanded the destruction and surrender
of what was precious to their worshipers. Primitive men
supposed that the first of the flock, the first of the field,
even the first-born child, ought to be offered up to their god.
Through the sacrifice of bulls and goats the god might be
made friendly to man. Even on the pages of the Old Testament we read of the worship at Jerusalem which was based
on the assumption that by the sprinkling of the blood of
precious animals on an altar access to God could be won.

If such ideas seem utterly strange and foreign to us, it is
due to the influence of Christian teaching. It completely
repudiated the idea that the blood of animals could bring
access to God. The author of the Epistle to the Hebrews
expressed the end of that kind of sacrificial religion by assert-
ing that the blood of Christ had once and for all abolished
all other blood offerings. What men could not do for them-

selves through their many sacrifices, God had done for them in the sacrifice of Christ. While much of the language of the old sacrificial religion is retained, the author makes a complete transformation. It is the obedience of Jesus, his self-giving for men, that constitutes his real sacrifice. "Lo, I come to do thy will." These words of the psalmist as transformed by the author of the Epistle to the Hebrews summed up the perfect sacrifice of Christ.

Christian faith has always held that the sacrifice of Christ was once and for all. But this does not mean that sacrifice is eliminated from religion. When genuine sacrifice is no longer required, religion has ceased to be the deepest expression of the human spirit. Every celebration of the Lord's Supper is a sacrifice. There is no adequate way to worship God except through sacrifice. Dreamy contemplation is not worship; nor is it sufficient to recall the sacrifice which someone else has made for us. If we are to worship truly, we too must make our offering. We must make a vital surrender to God.

According to ancient Christian custom there are three aspects of sacrificial offering in this service. First of all *we offer to God the bread and the wine* which we use in this act of worship. We ask for God's blessing upon the food, that in receiving it we may be fed with his heavenly feeding. But we do not think at first of his nourishment of our souls; it is our own sacrificial offering. The actual bread and wine represent almost no sacrifice on the part of the congregation. A loaf of bread and a bottle of grape juice could be donated to the church by any family without great sacrifice. In the Communion service they become sacramental symbols of Jesus' broken body. Now they are symbols of our economic life which we offer and surrender to God. All that goes into bread, which is representative of the necessities of life, and all that is signified by grape juice, which stands for the luxuries of life, we offer to God. If this sacrifice is to be genuine, it goes deep into the lives of every one of us.

In the second place *we offer to God our gifts to meet human need.* Traditionally the Communion offering was for the poor of the congregation. Today we have more thorough and effective ways of relieving poverty at home, thanks in large part to the spread of the ideals of the gospel. But we dare not lose from the Lord's Supper the expression of this form of sacrifice. It is indicative of the loss of this meaning that many churches do not have regular provision for a sacrificial offering as a part of this service. With hunger and need in so many parts of the world there should be a feeling of shame if any celebration omits a sacrificial offering for this purpose. The author of the Epistle to the Hebrews said: "Do not neglect to do good and to share what you have, for such sacrifices are pleasing to God." That is not less true today. In this service of worship we offer our gifts, not to keep up a temple establishment, but to feed God's poor in every land and to bind up their wounds.

In the third sacrifice we *offer to God praise and thanks-giving.* To the superficial mind this may appear as a cheap verbal substitute for some real sacrifice. But basically there is no offering which we can give to God which is greater than a deep gratitude for all that he has done for us. There are no *things* which we can give to God. All is from him, and he is not served by anything from human hands. But we can praise him who is the creator of all; we can thank him who has revealed his redeeming purpose throughout history and who in Christ has given us the truth which is the way to the life that is life eternal. This service is often called "Eucharist" from the Greek word for thanksgiving, and the sacrifice which we offer to God is one of thanksgiving. This is nothing easy; it means that we surrender all self-congratulation and self-sufficiency, and recognize our grateful dependence upon him.

After all these are not three separate offerings; they are woven into one strand in the act of our worship. They are various ways in which we would present ourselves—a spiritual sacrifice, which alone is acceptable to God. The perfect sacrifice of Jesus was a self-offering. If ours is to be like his, it too must be a self-sacrifice. We too may join in saying, "Lo, I come to do thy will." We come to offer unto him the sacrifice of ourselves.

The Fellowship of Communion

JOHN S. STAMM

God is faithful, by whom ye were called unto the
fellowship of his Son Jesus Christ our Lord.
—I Cor. 1:9

THE INSTITUTION AND PERPETUATION OF THE LORD'S SUP-
per in the Church clearly indicate that this is a service of
fellowship. On the night when Jesus instituted this sacrament, the occasion of the Passover Feast, he said that he
greatly desired this fellowship. Jesus wanted not only to
observe this historic feast but to establish a new service of
fellowship, a service commemorating the new covenant in
his blood. Fellowship is an integral part of the new life which
Christ gives. As Christians we are called into fellowship. The
promise is that if we walk in his light, as he is in the light,
we do have fellowship. This fellowship is with God and with
man. It issues from our spiritual birth. It is realized through
the cleansing from all unrighteousness and the constant
direction and inspiration of the Holy Spirit.

Man is made for fellowship. He can live fully and meaningfully only as he enters into the experience and practice of
fellowship. Man, however, seems often to be painfully
denied the enrichment of fellowship. He feels lonely, de-
pressed, and inhibited. He longs for fellowship, but it often
seems to elude him. Sin has robbed man of fellowship. It
has separated him from God and from men. One of the most

tragic aspects of human existence is this lack of fellowship with God and man. It not only robs man of his own highest and noblest life individually but also mars his group relationships. At the very root of world disorder today there is the lack of capacity for spiritually enriching fellowship.

The Lord's Supper is an abiding witness to the fact that God has undertaken to restore the bond of fellowship between God and man and between man and man. Through the life of Christ, and supremely through his sacrificial self-giving in death, the middle wall of partition that divides has been broken down and reconciliation has been made possible. God was in Christ reconciling the world unto himself. Through his Church he is now carrying forward the ministry of reconciliation. Through the atonement of Christ the estrangement is lifted, the enmity removed; and those who were afar off may freely enter his presence. Fellowship is made possible through the redemptive grace and power of God in Christ. In our observance of the Lord's Supper we affirm this great fact.

Through the birth of the Spirit man experiences the recovery of spiritual sonship. This implies an at-home feeling with God and a fellowship relationship with him in life and purpose. It creates hope, strength, and purpose and leads to a full devotion to Christ. Fellowship with God gives new meaning to all of life. It means guidance, assurance, comfort, and a sense of his presence which gives peace. It means salvation. It was this sense of comradeship which enabled the apostle Paul to say that if God is for us there is none who can prevail against us. Fellowship with God is the great privilege which all men may enjoy. In this fellowship there is a newness of life. This fellowship, however, is also a restoration of right relationships with man. The fellowship of believers is a vital element in the spiritual renewal through

Christ; it is a sense of comradeship with all who belong to Christ. It is a regulating and directing power in human relationships. It is one of the great needs of our day.

In the observance of Holy Communion there is a definite experience and expression of fellowship. The Church acknowledges the sacramental significance of this service. In a very special manner, designed by Christ himself, this service is a unique means of grace to quicken, nourish, and strengthen the spiritual life of the participant. The manner and measure of the mediation of this grace is, however, differently interpreted. There are those who believe this is accomplished through a physical sharing, others through a veiled physical presence, others through a spiritual sharing. But all accept this service as a unique impartation of redemptive grace and power. Whatever the interpretation, the Lord's Supper is accepted by the Christian Church as a service of fellowship. It is a witness to the truth that fellowship is real.

The service of Holy Communion is a constant reminder of the love of God. Sin made the cross necessary, but only the love of God made the cross possible. As we receive the consecrated emblems, we are reminded of the broken body and the shed blood. Jesus' own interpretation of his sacrificial self-giving in death was that God loved the world and therefore gave his Son. The love of God is the basic element in revelation. In love God disclosed himself to man. In love he entered into redemptive relationship with sinful man. In love he made the great sacrifice through his Son. Love is always most fully revealed in sacrificial social-mindedness. The love of God is most perfectly revealed on the cross.

It is this assurance of the love of God that men need. There is much in this world which does not suggest love. There is much hate, bitterness, strife, unbrotherliness, and death. Men often long for the touch of a loving hand. The Lord's Supper is a service in and through which men are assured there is love. God does love. He does care. He commits himself to man in love. He shares in love. In his love there is comfort, healing, and peace. He loves all men. He gave his Son in love that whosoever believeth might have life. But he loves the individual. The marvelous truth is that each one may say, "He loves even me."

God not only assures us of his love; through the Holy Spirit he sheds abroad in the hearts of believers his own love so that they too may enter into a life of love. Holy Communion means sharing in the grace and power made available in love. Such love as God manifested in the gift of Christ must call forth love in us. We can help God heal the wounds of sin and establish a fellowship of love. We can bring cheer and comfort to those who are lonely and afraid. We can lift horizons and bring courage and hope. Such a life of sacrificial self-giving needs constant quickening and strengthening through the reassurance of the love of God. The Lord's Supper is a service supremely designed to remind us that God loves.

The service of Holy Communion is a constant reminder of the inexhaustible resource made available for man through the love of God. The apostle Paul was so overwhelmed with this thought that he said that since God spared not his Son but gave him for us, surely he will also freely give us all things. God gave his Son not only to deliver man from the power and dominion of sin but also to bring him into fullness of life. He has made atonement for man's sin and now seeks to impart the riches of his grace that man may live fully and meaningfully.

Man needs such assurance. He has aspirations, but often these are seemingly defeated through loss of resource. When

I was a lad on a farm in Kansas, I heard my father say that if he had had the money when he first arrived in that place he could have purchased a tract of land adjoining our farm for a nominal price. This seemed such a desirable addition to our farm that I often wondered why one should be deprived of such a good by lack of resources. I have since learned that often such things happen. Men are limited and deprived of many things which seem to lie in the path of their progress. We are in a world where no one is assured an inexhaustible supply in terms of things. Much has been done to make possible better sharing. Much still needs to be done. A full supply of things will always elude men. Not so in things spiritual. God is withholding nothing which man needs to rise to the highest heights as a spiritual personality. He has made available to all the resources of his grace. He wants to share with men. He will supply every need. Nothing good will be withheld. In God there is all that man needs for abundant life. As we share in the Lord's Supper, we are reminded that he who gave will withhold no good thing.

The service of Holy Communion is the call of God for men to respond to this love and share in this resource. Christ has commanded his followers to observe the Communion as a remembrance of what God has done and will do. He invites us to share in this fellowship. If men are to share, there must be a wholehearted acceptance of the purposes of God.

God is often unable to give because man is not worthy to receive. A pastor was called to a home one evening to counsel with troubled parents. With much difficulty and deep emotion the father presented their great sorrow. With tears streaming down he said, "I have accumulated a business. Mother and I have now come to the years when we feel we should step out of active work and pass this business over to our son. Our son, however, is not trustworthy, and we cannot give him what we have for him." As the heart of this father was grieved that he could not give what his love prompted him to give, so the heart of God must be grieved because so often men are not trustworthy. We are therefore commanded, before we receive the consecrated emblems, to prove ourselves, to examine ourselves that we may participate worthily. The observance of the Lord's Supper is a call to self-examination and to renewed commitment to Christ and his cause. We can share in this holy fellowship only if we are in accord with God.

If men are to share, there must be participation. It is tragic that many neglect, and even reject, the redemptive grace and power of God, and thus stand outside of this privilege. We need to rekindle the spirit of evangelism and missions in the Church. Men need to be won to Christ and his cause. They need to become sharers of his grace. But it is also tragic that many who profess Christ are often indifferent to the means of grace offered in and through the Lord's Supper. That is why they lack spiritual renewal and enrichment. To neglect this observance is not only to be disobedient to the command of Christ but also to be spiritually impoverished. Christ has instituted this service for spiritual enrichment. We should faithfully share in its blessings.

If men are to share, they must also be deeply concerned about translating into thought, life, and conduct the spiritual character and purpose of this service. Men must share not only at the Lord's Table; they must share in all of life. The fellowship of Communion must become a fellowship of life. Our redemption must be expressed through character and service. We can share meaningfully only at the table of the Lord as we share with him our lives.

A Fellowship Without Frontiers

JESSE M. BADER

*And they continued stedfastly in the . . . fellow-
ship.* —Acts 2:42

A<small>T AMSTERDAM WHEN THE WORLD COUNCIL OF CHURCHES</small>
was organized in the summer of 1948, a Communion
service was held in the Nieuwe Kerk, just across the
street from the palace of the queen of Holland. Over
one thousand delegates and visitors, representing the majority of the nations of the earth and the major Protestant
groups of the world, came together and knelt at the Lord's
Table to partake of the Holy Communion. As they sat
together in this deeply reverent service, everyone present
was impressed by a sense of fellowship with Christ and with
all Christians throughout the world. The whole service
seemed aglow with his divine Presence. Again "he was
known of them in breaking of bread."

The greatest thing about the early Christians was not
their wealth. For the most part they were poor. They
were not distinguished for their scholastic training. Most
of them were unlettered. They were not known for their
high social position in the Roman world. Most of them
belonged to the working class. There was one distinguishable
characteristic by which they were known—fellowship. Pentecost had separated these early disciples of Jesus Christ into

ono 93 ono

a Church and bound them together in an unbreakable fellowship. On Pentecost it was said of them that "they were all with one accord in one place." It is comparatively easy to get Christians in one place, but to get them in one place "with one accord" is difficult. The fellowship of the early Christians was a fellowship of faith. Not only did they belong to something; they believed something. Their fellowship was a fellowship of suffering. Every footprint in the book of Acts is stained with blood. Nothing happened easily. Their fellowship was a fellowship of prayer. They advanced on their knees. Prayer is mentioned twenty-nine times in the book of Acts. And also their fellowship was a fellowship of love. They possessed the compassionate heart. They cared. They provided for the widows and orphans. They fed the hungry. They were so different from those about them that they were looked upon as a third race. They were a fellowship.

One of the greatest needs today within the total Church of our Lord Jesus Christ is the restoration of the New Testament fellowship. Where can this fellowship of Christians be more vividly expressed than at the Lord's Table? There is no scandal in the fact that Lutherans and Calvinists do not have precisely the same understanding of the Lord's Supper. The scandal, however, is that they therefore cannot celebrate the communion with each other, which indeed amounts to this, that they do not acknowledge each other to be the Church.

But increasingly Christians are removing fences and breaking down walls that hinder fellowship. Robert Frost put it forcefully when he said:

> Something there is that doesn't like a wall.
> That wants it down.

Walls separate and divide. Most Christians don't like them, and they rebel against them. The removal process is going on at a rapid pace, and Christian fellowship is flowing back and forth across denominational lines. A larger, richer fellowship within the total Church is taking place. This is seen in the organization of the World Council of Churches, in the co-operative work of the Federal Council of Churches, and in the unity of effort found in 727 state, county, and city Councils of Churches in America. A new day has come among the churches in the area of closer co-operation, finer unity, and deeper appreciation of each other. Even inter-communion is not many years away. The fellowship of Christians about the Lord's Table is a fellowship without frontiers. All are one in Jesus Christ, and in him all are brethren.

> In Christ there is no East or West
> In Him no South or North;
> But one great fellowship of love
> Throughout the whole wide earth.

This fellowship about the Lord's Table has amazing dimensions. Have you ever thought how far-reaching it is? This fellowship reaches upward to God through Jesus Christ our Lord. At this holy table we are reminded of our unforgettable relationship to God in the verse, "God so loved the world, that he gave his only begotten Son, that whosoever believeth in him should not perish, but have everlasting life." This fellowship is perpendicular. It reaches to the very heart of a redemptive and loving God, for "God was in Christ, reconciling the world unto himself."

This fellowship reaches back through that long line of believers which began at the first observance in the upper room in the long ago. Did John, the beloved disciple, receive it first from the hands of his Lord? If so, he has handed it on to a faithful company. Think of that glorious company —the early fathers of the Church, the writers of the Christian literature of the ages, the great poets, artists, reformers, statesmen, rulers, missionaries, martyrs, and many others— who have gathered about this holy table down the centuries. This long line reaches back into the past, bringing us into fellowship with those who now dwell with Christ in the land of an unsetting sun. It is an unbroken and an unbreakable line of those who have loved and served him. These belong to the Church triumphant.

This fellowship reaches far *outward* in the present. It enfolds a great multitude of living witnesses in all parts of the world. At the Lord's Table a Christian is in fellowship with them. Represented at his table are many languages, different races, and many nations. Here at last we are not divided—not by race, speech, or color. This is the most widespread religious observance of the world, and each Christian is a part of it. Each Christian Church body, with few exceptions, treasures this table as its own, with its one Host, Jesus Christ. Here we forget our differences, remembering only him and the widespread brotherhood of believers into which he brings us. Through this broken body we become one body. This fellowship is inclusive.

World Communion Sunday brings vividly to mind the outward reaches of our fellowship. The "Table of Remembrance" is spread first with its sacred emblems by those churches living just beyond the international date line— Fiji Islands, New Zealand, Australia, and others. Annually on the first Sunday in October this table is 25,000 miles long. How inspiring and strengthening to belong to such a fellowship. All meet in him.

In Christ now meet both East and West
In Him meet South and North;
All Christly souls are one in Him
Throughout the whole wide earth.

And the fellowship reaches forward. Let us rejoice in the assurance that after we have gone into the Presence, others will be coming after us to take their places in this unending fellowship on earth and in heaven. They too will take their places at this table to remember him whom Paul spoke of when he said, "For as often as ye eat this bread, and drink this cup, ye do shew the Lord's death till he come." Christians partake of his triumph, and they live and work in the power and hope of his coming victory.

To perpetuate this fellowship Christians must go forth from the holy table to be his witnesses, and to so witness by life, words, and deeds that others may be persuaded to accept Jesus Christ as Lord and Saviour. In this way the Church is strengthened spiritually and numerically. The timeless mandate of our Lord Jesus Christ is, "Go make disciples." As Christians go forth from his Table of Remembrance, it should be to bear an unmistakable witness in behalf of him whom they love and serve. "Let the redeemed of the Lord say so" is a clarion call to all disciples to make more and better disciples.

As a part of this fellowship without frontiers all Christians in this time of tension and uncertainty are called upon to make a new dedication of life. All areas of life in each of us need to be surrendered to him who said, "The Son of man came not to be ministered unto, but to minister, and to give his life a ransom for many." In his spirit, life should be expendable. He should have all there is of us. Anything less than that is unworthy of those who belong to this fellowship without frontiers.

One evening Fritz Kreisler, the noted violinist, was being entertained in the home of some wealthy people. After the dinner the family assembled in the living room. The mother of the home seated herself at the piano. The father brought out a beautiful Cremona violin and handed it to Kreisler. After he had tuned the instrument, he swept the strings for an hour. He handed the violin back to the owner; but the owner refused it, saying, "From now on the instrument belongs to you. You are the one who can bring the best out of it." We belong to Christ and to a fellowship without frontiers. We are his, and as Christians we belong together. He is the one, and the only one, who can bring the best out of us.

Communion Chairs

EDWIN T. DAHLBERG

*For where two or three are gathered together in
my name, there am I in the midst of them.*
—Matt. 18:20

Henry david thoreau in his best-known book,
Walden, said concerning the furnishings of his wilderness
hut on the shores of the Walden Pond: "I had three chairs
in my house; one for solitude, two for friendship, three for
society." As we are furnishing our homes and churches
today, are we making room for these three chairs?

Jesus made it quite clear, for example, that for vital,
personal communion with God we need the *chair of solitude.* "But thou, when thou prayest," he said, "enter into
thine inner chamber, and having shut thy door, pray to thy
Father who is in secret, and thy Father who seeth in secret
shall recompense thee" (Matt. 6:6 A.S.V.). He practiced
this personal communion consistently. He prayed by the
shores of Galilee when the setting sun was turning the waters
of the lake to liquid gold. He spent long nights alone in the
mountains.

In these days of consternation and confusion we need
more than ever a time and place where we can meditate,
ruminate, and think God's thoughts after him. So many
things jangle our nerves during the day. It has been well said

that if Thomas Gray were to write today his "Elegy Written in a Country Churchyard," he would entitle it "Elegy Written in a City Freight Yard." In the midst of the din and clamor of modern life to sit down in the chair of solitude, whether outdoors or indoors, is to receive once again the balm of Gilead, which alone can heal the sin-sick soul and make the wounded whole.

Thoreau said that although he did not have a drawing room, he did have a "with-drawing room." This best room was the pine wood back of his house, where the shadows were so deep and still that the sunlight could barely thrust its way through. The floor was carpeted with pine needles. And a priceless domestic—the wind, the sun, and the rain— "swept the floor and dusted the furniture and kept the things in order."

There is probably nothing that could bring quite so much blessing to our souls as a sense of the Holy in some solitary place that has been well called "a room of one's own." There we learn "that the big things are big, and the little things little, before it is too late."

We should not be discouraged by the fact that even in solitude we suffer so many interruptions that we sometimes feel a lack of success in prayer. In the book *A Sense of the Holy* a sixteenth-century mystic is reported to have said:

When we consider the manifold weakness of the strongest devotions in time of prayer, it is a sad consideration. I throw myself down in my chamber, and I call in and invite God and his angels thither, and when they are there I neglect God and his angels for the noise of a fly, for the rustling of a coach, for the whining of a door; I talk on—knees bowed down as though I prayed to God; and if God and his angels should ask me when I thought of God last in that prayer, I cannot tell.

Although our trysts with God are so intimate and personal that it would be a violation of divine confidence to relate all that he speaks to us there, I can bear personal testimony that nothing so strengthens the soul as does the hour spent in the chair of solitude. In spite of the interruptions, in spite of the wandering thoughts and the ineptitude in prayer, we rise from such an hour saying as did the psalmist of old: "Why art thou cast down, O my soul? and why art thou disquieted within me? hope thou in God: for I shall yet praise him, who is the health of my countenance, and my God."

If in the home of the spirit we have the chair of solitude, however, we need equally *two chairs for friendship*. The person who spends all his prayer life alone will end up by being queer. He needs to supplement his solitude, therefore, with friendship.

A friend of mine once stayed in the home of a minister who spent practically the whole week in his study reading his Bible and praying. One day my friend said to him, "You are to be commended for your devotions. But I have noticed that in the whole week I have been here, not one young person of your congregation has come in to see you. Nor have your own children come." This man was queer. He limited himself so completely to the chair of solitude that he forgot the chairs of friendship.

How heartening are the words of Jesus, "I have called you friends!" And his other remark to the disciples, "Ye are they which have continued with me in my temptations."

Every one of us can have friends if he will follow a simple principle of friendship. This principle is to seek out those who are more lonesome, bashful, or embarrassed than he, rather than to strive for the companionship of those he feels to be above himself. I was brought up in the country. When we moved to the city, I did not know how to play the group games of city children. I had spent more of my time playing in the fields or snaring gophers. So I used to stand forlornly beside the schoolhouse wall, wishing that I knew how to play baseball, run-sheep-run, and other games. Fortunately I got over that and learned to participate with the others. But through the years I have learned that if we befriend those whom others have forgotten, and pay attention to people whom others dislike or pass by, there is developed within us some magnetic power by which we attract delightful friendships to ourselves, provided that we obey what the late Henry Churchill King in his book *The Meaning of Friendship* declared to be the three basic laws of friendship: (1) Time. Unless we give time to our friends, we cannot retain them nor keep our friendship alive. (2) Sacrifice. If we make no sacrifices for our friends but expect rather that they should make all the sacrifices for us, there can be no continuing relationship of affection and comradeship. (3) Mutual Interests. Whether it be music, work, travel, or religion, the deepest friendships require something in common.

These laws of friendship hold true for the divine as well as the human friendships. We can be friends of Jesus only as we give time to Christ, make sacrifices for him as he has made an eternal sacrifice on Calvary for us, and engage in interests that are mutual with his own. May it not be that our coldness and indifference to Christianity today are due to the fact that none of the interests that we consider primary are interests of Jesus at all? His great interests were mercy, truth, and righteousness; the love of God, the children of God, the kingdom of God.

Recently I had a wonderful reunion with a fellow pastor whom I had not seen for many years but with whom I had barnstormed all the way up and down the Pacific Coast from Seattle to San Francisco and on through Arizona to El Paso as his comrade in a preaching mission for one of our home mission societies. One night just a few weeks ago I was to speak at a meeting in Chicago. What was my delight to find him sitting across the table from me at the dinner. We chuckled and laughed, as old friends do, over the jolly things we had done together in past years, and then we grew serious as we learned of the intervening sorrow. He had lost two of his four children in their youth. After the war one of his sons had been killed in a plane crash at Oak Ridge, leaving only one remaining son. Following this tragedy my friend had had a serious heart attack, but had recovered sufficiently to resume his pulpit. So the night of the Chicago program he was to give the devotional message. He seemed so frail and his face so flushed. Immediately after he had spoken, he left the platform and disappeared so that we did not have a chance to say good-by. What was my dismay to learn that just two days later his heart failed him, and he died instantly! But none of us who heard him that night will forget his last message or the radiant smile with which he looked around at us as he repeated over and over again, "We are here because we are the friends of Jesus."

That is why we gather together in the church from Sunday to Sunday, and assemble on the Lord's Day at the Communion table. We are the friends of Jesus. Do you have a chair in your home for him?

But as there is the one chair of solitude, and there are the two chairs for friendship, there should be also the *three chairs for society.*

This is one of the basic meanings of the communion service; we are members of a Christian society. Salvation is not personal alone. It is corporate also. Except we are members of the Church and are worshiping and working together in the universal fellowship of Christ's kingdom, we have not sensed the whole significance of the gospel.

It is interesting to note that according to the teachings of our faith there are even three chairs in the Godhead. According to the doctrine of the Trinity we speak of God the Father, God the Son, and God the Holy Spirit. It is as though even in Deity there must be society as well as solitude—a great fellowship of joy.

One of the most necessary discoveries of the Christian faith today is that of community. It is not enough that we have enjoyable little circles of friendship or family relationships, "We four and no more." Even in the church people often make a mistake by so limiting themselves to a group, whether it be the choir or a Sunday-school class or a women's circle, that they miss the significance of that wider religious society we know as a church. And within the church itself we can become so preoccupied with our parish and parochial interests that we forget the wider family of mankind and never experience what John Wollman felt when he said that he had been "baptized into a feeling of the conditions of the people."

On Sunday, December 7, 1941, the American people were stunned as they listened to their radios and heard the news of Pearl Harbor. December 14, the week following, was International Bible Sunday. As members of the First Baptist Church in Washington, D.C., settled in their seats for the eleven o'clock service, the pastor, Dr. Edward H. Pruden, the pastor of President Truman, entered with a Japanese, a Chinese, a German, a Russian, an Englishman, and an Italian.

Each of these in turn read John 3:16 from the pulpit in his native tongue: "For God so loved the world, that he gave his only begotten Son, that whosoever believeth in him should not perish, but have everlasting life." The service then proceeded as usual.

The purpose of this international prelude to the service that Sunday was to remind the people present that no matter what might happen, not even war itself could destroy the bonds of Christian fellowship that hold the community of Jesus Christ together. What a glorious testimony!

It was such a testimony to the reconciling society of Christ our Saviour that was given supremely in 1948 at the Amsterdam Assembly of the World Council of Churches, where 148 denominations were gathered together from 44 different countries.

I remember that as we came together in successive groups of one hundred at the white, cloth-covered tables in the Nieuwe Kerk the second Sunday of the assembly, a pastor from a different denomination and race and nationality officiated for each group. What impressed us most at the point where the fifth group of one hundred came forward was that the young minister administering the elements of the Lord's Supper was a native of Indonesia. Next to him at his right sat a Dutch layman, a member of the Dutch Parliament—a member, indeed, of the Conservative party in the Dutch Parliament, which had been the stiffest in its opposition to the liberation of the Indonesian Republic. As the dark-faced young Indonesian pastor lifted his hands in blessing over the cup and said so tenderly, "The blood of Jesus Christ, shed for thee," the first one to whom he handed the cup was the member of the Dutch Parliament. It was as though in the passing of that cup from the Indonesian's hand to the Dutch layman's hand there was the dissolving of every barrier of politics, nationality, race, and empire.

And so it was all around the table. On my left were two

Chinese delegates and a black-bearded youth delegate from
Syria, across the table a bishop of the Anglican Church in
Australia. Next to him were two Negro delegates from the
United States, side by side with a woman from India. Next
to her was a fine Christian woman from Africa with the
tribal marks of her people still deeply scarred in her face.
As the great silver goblet went silently from hand to hand
around that sacred table, we could here again the words of
Jesus, saying, "This do in remembrance of me." It was the
Christian community in its very essence, so vibrant with
the joy of an everlasting fellowship that we could truly say,
"Christ is risen. He is risen indeed!"

As the Amsterdam message expresses it, "We are coming
together. We intend to stay together."

One chair for solitude—yes. And two chairs for friendship. But three chairs—chairs without number—for society
—the affectionate society of Jesus Christ.

God's Invitation—Man's Response

E. G. HOMRIGHAUSEN

The kingdom of heaven is like unto a certain king, which made a marriage for his son, and sent forth his servants to call them that were bidden to the wedding, . . . saying, Tell them which are bidden . . . all things are ready: come unto the marriage.—Matt. 22:2-4

IN ONE OF JESUS' REMARKABLE STORIES HE TOLD OF A KING who prepared a wedding feast for his son. Though the invitations went out by personal messengers, not only did the would-be guests refuse to come, but some of the messengers were shamefully and spitefully treated, even killed. When this report reached the king's ear, he sent his military forces to wreak vengeance upon the culprits. Then he sent out a general invitation to all whom the servants could persuade to come to the wedding feast. Among the guests there was one who did not wear a wedding garment. He was ushered from the party and in disgrace cast into outer darkness.

As we study this story, we see the accuracy with which it describes the ways of God with men, the response of men to God, the consequences of man's attitudes toward God. It is not an overstatement to say that the essence of the gospel is found in this story.

The Gospels take for granted that God *always takes the initiative.* What God does is always the important matter.

He is the first and the last, the one upon whom all else depends. This is what makes the Christian faith unique. The eternal God, by whose will all things were brought forth and by whose continued care all things are sustained, has provided something wonderful for us. He has sought to bring real happiness into human life by dignifying it and setting it within eternal dimensions. While he is the God of the universe, he is also the God of the individual person. This gospel of ours is good news about what God is, has done, and is doing to provide for us. The men of our time are earth-bound; their eyes are turned toward the human. Their despair is caused by the limitation of their vision. But if God be for us, who can be against us? Because God has done something unprecedented for us, life may be different; doors of great possibility may be open to us.

The things men do are transient. In spite of the brilliance of Greek, Roman, and Egyptian civilizations, they are no longer alive. We cannot fulfill our lives by our own strength. We cannot achieve the goals which we set for ourselves. The evidence of this fact is apparent in this day of tragedy, conflict, and war.

Men are becoming aware of the fact that they must look beyond human ingenuity for the things that abide. Christianity affirms that either there is a personal God or life is meaningless. It is upon him that we must depend for our hopes. It is not enough to believe in a supreme Power behind all things. We must believe in a God who has purpose and character, a God who knows us and loves us and with whom we may have eternal fellowship. It is faith in this personal God which we manifest when we participate in the sacrament of the Lord's Supper. Men did not invent this feast; it was instituted for us through Christ in the name of and by the authority of God.

What does God provide men? What does Christianity have to offer? God's action on our behalf is as a wedding feast. The table is laden with many choice delicacies to satisfy the most fastidious appetite. But there is more. There is music, laughter, fellowship with the people we like, fellowship with the gracious Host. It is around him that we meet, and only through his generosity are we present at all. That which God wishes, above all else, is fellowship with his children and fellowship among the people of the earth in his name. What else does communion mean? What else does reconciliation mean? The purpose of God-in-Christ is that harmony may prevail in earth and heaven. Prodigals are to come home, and brothers within the home are to live by the laws of love. God's will is peace between men and himself and between men and men.

It was for this reason that Jesus instituted the memorial of the Last Supper. It was to be an experience of the real fellowship which he came to establish on earth. Those gathering around his table should feel a sense of communion with God and with each other. A new relationship should come into existence. His table should be the center of a new humanity in the earth. Around this table should be the representative Church universal and eternal.

It is to this sort of supper that men are invited. By various messengers we are bidden to share in the provision which God has made for us. Yet God cannot force us to partake of his generosity. His love can be received only in a responding faith. The Lord's Supper is our possibility made available by the gracious invitation of God, who has no other desire than that men may find the things which belong to their peace and welfare.

The responses which men offered to the king's invitation were not only disappointing, but insulting and dangerous.

Jesus was not exaggerating the reactions of men to God's gracious overture. He knew what was in the heart of man. He himself was to feel the effect of man's inhumanity to man and man's insolence toward God. This is one of the enigmas of history: man has the power to reject truth, kill justice, and crucify love. Why should God grant unto men the gift of freedom, the abuse of which can undo his work and thwart his purposes? The saints have wondered at the patience of God.

The invited guest regretfully declined in some instances; in other instances they treated the messengers with such violence that they were killed. Can this be true to history? Were not many of the prophets stoned to death? What happened to Jesus? To the early Christians? To those who, today, call the Church back from traditionalism to a vital simple faith?

Modern psychologists have much to say about the way men treat those who seek to help them. Men with deep resentments will sometimes "take it out" on those who love them most. Truth seems such an enemy to one who is untruthful. Love is hateful to those who are not in love. Men hate the Christ, who threatens their selfishness and pride.

Those who refused to come to the wedding feast were not atheists. No doubt they were respectable people who believed in and supported religion. But they assumed that their religious interests should never interfere with their other interests in life. How many assume the same thing today? Most people are not completely evil; they simply neglect or ignore the good. They "make light" of God and the divine order and offer. Do not we all seek to make excuses? While we are not created to be monks and world-withdrawing ascetics, we are asked to "seek . . . first the kingdom of God, and his righteousness," and we so often find ourselves putting primary considerations in second place. To "make heavy" of this world's goods is but to "make light" of the things that abide.

The consequences of such neglect are disastrous. The continuous quest for mundane goals reduces life to the level of the animal. It means the death of personality, the core of which is the image of God made new by the grace of God. The "wrath of God" is no arbitrary doctrine preached to the world by gloomy churchmen; it is the inevitable law of rejected love. If the "elect" desire their birthright, the stage is set for tragedy. And if the classes fail to take God seriously, they will be rejected in favor of the masses. For God's purpose will not be thwarted. God's house will be filled with guests, though they may not be those who received the original invitations. The destroyed peoples and the burned cities of our day are ample proof to us that those who reject the King's offer will themselves be rejected.

The invitation goes to all men. And men have in all ages responded. We do not sit alone at the Lord's Supper. There are millions who sit at the same feast. They come from all the nations of the earth, and their voices are blended in happy song and friendly conversation. Thank God there is a Church that sings:

> Elect from every nation,
> Yet one o'er all the earth.

Among those who came to the king's supper there was one who was not properly attired. In those days it is said the king would send, along with the invitation, the wedding garments to be worn. While this man had accepted the invitation, he had taken lightly the accepted dress. Others knew what they had rejected; this man did not adequately understand what he had accepted. He did not realize that those who accept the King's invitation cannot remain as they are. The old Adam simply cannot barge into the company of those who are expected to put on the "new man in Christ," the man who is born again. He was as the man who has the form of religion but denies the essence thereof. This man masqueraded—unconsciously—as a member of the wedding party, yet he did not know what it was about. Outwardly he was present at the Lord's Table, but inwardly he was a stranger to its meaning. He wanted new life but did not fill the qualifications for its appropriation. He believed but did not obey.

No one can remain undetected who comes to God's feast in such a condition. He is eliminated by the inexorable law of reality, and his ultimate end is darkness and pain. This is the result of those who say "yes" but live "no." It is the judgment of those who think they can come into God's grace clothed with the soiled garments of the world. They would enjoy the feast, but they would not change their habits. They want both God and mammon. Ultimately the judgment of God catches up with them, and they find themselves in a world of darkness and pain.

Many are called, but few are chosen. While there is a wideness in God's mercy, it is offered in vain to many people. Some of the modern messengers of God have suffered the firing squad of the concentration camps. The way that leads to eternal life is narrow, and there are few that travel it. Yet we are thankful to God for those who accept his invitation and wear the garments that befit their dignity and status. They adorn themselves with the life that expresses their characters. They enter into a divine fellowship.

At the table of our Lord we engage in something high and

holy. We express something which is eternally abiding and universally relevant. What we do there is symbolic of what God wishes the whole world to be—a happy people whose sins are forgiven and whose lives are filled with the dignity of the children of God. It is the Lord's table; it is God's provision, his way of revealing to us his holy passion for a redeemed world. Let us accept his invitation and go into his royal house properly attired in the garments of genuine humility and joyous faith!

The Power of a Look

G. RAY JORDAN

*And the Lord turned, and looked upon Peter. And
Peter remembered . . . and . . . went out, and wept
bitterly.* —Luke 22:61-62

W HO CAN EVER HOPE TO DESCRIBE THE FACE OF JESUS
when he turned and looked upon Simon Peter? Of course
the Master was keenly disappointed. But we can also be
sure his countenance showed compassion, tenderness, and
forgiveness. This one look may have saved Peter from the
experience of Judas. What was bitter remorse for the latter
became genuine, wholehearted repentance for the former.
Many of us are familiar with both emotions.

All of us know something of the power of looks, whether
they are pleasant and friendly or reproving and antagonistic.
We have felt the influence of both the winsome smile of
love and the glare of hate.

We are aware that a glance is often far more effective
than a spoken word. We know the force of facial expressions.
We are influenced by the gaze of the curious, the stare of
the unfriendly, the scornful frown of our critics, the friendly
smile of encouragement from one who loves us.

Eyes that search us have penetrating power. There are
eyes which seem to follow us even after their owner with-
draws from our presence. There are eyes that twinkle, eyes

that dance, eyes that talk, eyes that entreat us to be friends, eyes that tell us we are loved.

Sometimes when one stares at us, he may be questioning us. He may be trying to read our thoughts. He may not necessarily be unfriendly. By a look he is asking what is on our minds.

There are looks which are markedly unfriendly. It is most unpleasant to realize that one who does not like you is frowning at you. We say such a person is looking "daggers" at us. Even new acquaintances may give us a "withering" look.

A lover fastens his gaze upon the face of his beloved. Here is eloquence that words cannot express. In an hour when we are about to collapse someone in whom we believe turns and looks at us with hope and faith, in confidence and trust. A mother may look at a child tenderly and kindly even when she shows keen disappointment. A glance like that often remains with one throughout life.

Sometimes we receive great inspiration because of the way someone looks at us. A friend seems to say, "You can do it! Make a try! I am for you!" What strength that gives us. We gain confidence in ourselves. We feel like starting over again. In this way Christians learn to share their assurance of God's gracious gift of forgiveness and spiritual strength.

Most of us can remember how our mothers helped us to have faith by their very looks. Undoubtedly the way Mary looked at Jesus when he was a boy had something to do with his words on the cross, "Woman, behold thy Son! . . . Behold thy mother!"

Jesus knew the power of eyes. When he looked at Simon Peter after his denial, he demonstrated this spiritual force. The tender glance of keen disappointment cut this hardened fisherman to the heart. But it also gave him hope. It did not speak harsh reproof. It disclosed pathetic disappointment. Simon could have stood the former; the latter he could not stand. It was this loving look of pain and of disappointment that saved Simon Peter. He remembered what Jesus said: "Simon, Simon, behold, Satan hath desired to have you, that he might sift you like wheat: but I have prayed for thee, that thy faith fail not: and when thou art converted, strengthen thy brethren." He recalled his own protest: "Lord, I am ready to go with thee, both into prison and to death." And then there were the words of the Master: "This night, before the cock crow, thou shalt deny me thrice."

Simon knew what the eyes of Jesus were saying. He knew that the Master was disappointed in him but that he still loved him—and trusted him. That made Peter's memory of the Last Supper unforgettably vivid. He recalled Jesus' anticipation of betrayal, denial, and death. It was like another Holy Communion, for not only did Jesus communicate with him; he sustained him by a look.

On another day Jesus revealed the piercing power of his eyes. It was when he looked upon some men who had brought a guilty woman in his presence, expecting condemnation for her. At first the Master did not even glance at the woman. But when he had spoken in a clear-cut and searching manner, the flash of his eyes swept the crowd. They could never forget that! One glance had scorched the very consciences of these guilty churchmen!

We too have eyes—not merely eyes to see Jesus as he sits at the table for holy fellowship, but eyes with which we can learn to look as he did. No matter how casually or thoughtlessly we look at things, there are inescapable consequences in those looks. The part of our evironment which most influences us is that to which we make some response.

Our answer of interest becomes one of the determining factors in making and shaping our lives. Sometimes that is the result of a hurried glance which we thoughtlessly give some unworthy or repulsive painting. Sometimes the most sordid sights imaginable enter our minds through the eye gate.

A young man visited one of the degraded sections of one of our large cities. This youth insisted that he wanted to see life as it actually was. Well, he had his look. But it made an impression of such horror upon him, so etched its ugliness on his heart and wrote its sordid message so deeply upon his soul, that later he declared he would glady give anything within the bounds of reason to erase it from his mind. But the image had registered upon the photographic plate of his soul.

Few of us understand how seriously we are affected by that upon which we fasten our attention. All that we see affects us: the billboards on the highway, the movies on the screens, the photographs and pictures in the books and magazines which we read. If we look at these long enough, their character impresses itself upon our minds and hearts. We are a part of all we meet—with eyes and memory. Most of the advertisements, signs, and books are for this very purpose. They become a constant mental environment for us.

That is why we should take time to look at Christ before we partake of the Holy Communion. This look may deliver us from a shameful past and save us from a regrettable future.

Christ's beauty, truth, and bravery may write their messages on our minds and hearts. These are in the eyes of Jesus as he faces us during Communion. They become ours if we look devotedly in his face as we sit with him in the upper room. We can see divine daring and ardent affection in his eyes and we have fellowship with him in hours of Holy Communion.

Wordsworth in his poem "I Wandered Lonely as a Cloud" understood the mighty force of spiritual vision even as it had to do with the visible world. It was about this he was thinking when he wrote:

> I wandered lonely as a cloud
> That floats on high o'er vales and hills,
> When all at once I saw a crowd,
> A host, of golden daffodils;
> Beside the lake, beneath the trees,
> Fluttering and dancing in the breeze.
>
> .   .   .   .
>
> For oft, when on my couch I lie
> In vacant or in pensive mood,
> They flash upon that inward eye
> Which is the bliss of solitude;
> And then my heart with pleasure fills,
> And dances with the daffodils.

Thus what some people call a mere dream world becomes one of the great realities of life. Bess Streeter Aldrich has reminded us of this in the volume *A Lantern in Her Hand*. In one of the chapters she describes how Will, the husband, laughs at some of his wife's ideas. "You're quite a dreamer, Abbie girl," he says. But Abbie does not laugh. Suddenly she becomes sober.

"You have to, Will," she says a bit vehemently. "You have to dream things out. It keeps a kind of an ideal before you. You see it first in your mind and then you set about to try to make it like the ideal. If you want a garden—why, I guess you're got to dream a garden."

Jesus saw a world redeemed. He dreamed about it. He dared to make his dreams come true. He would not surrender his hopes and his faith even as he faced Gethsemane and the Cross. He was thinking of those in the upper room. We too can develop the art of using our spiritual eyes. The unseen becomes quite real. We see with our souls!

> O world invisible, we view thee,
> O world intangible, we touch thee,
> O world unknowable, we know thee,
> Inapprehensible, we clutch thee! [1]

This is one of the vivid and vital experiences of high religion. It helps us understand what Jesus meant when he declared, "Yet a little while, and the world seeth me no more; but ye see me: because I live, ye shall live also." It will also explain those notable words, "Moses wist not that the skin of his face shone." It will interpret the words, "He endured, as seeing him who is invisible." Eyes, imagination, and the vision of the soul—what power there is here!

So we lift our eyes to the everlasting hills. We respond to the winsome appeal of love in the eyes of Christ. We put God in the central place of our lives. The truest desires of our souls become realities. Our eyes are opened! The scales that blind us to the eternal drop away. We see reality! That is why we ask "no dream, no prophet ecstasies." We do not seek a "sudden rending of the veil of clay." We do not hopefully anticipate an angel visitant or an opening of the skies. We do earnestly pray, "Lord, take the dimness of my soul away."

Only as we come to see the Divine can there be peace, inner quietude, and confidence. The promise of spiritual

[1] From "In No Strange Land" by Francis Thompson.

vision is for those who know how to live and worship. "Blessed are the pure in heart: for they shall see God."

At its best worship is holding high some great truth and saying, "See!" Always it reminds us of reality to which we are to give ourselves. Indeed, the truest worship is looking toward the *Unseen* and saying, "*See!*" But we have to decide to look for ourselves. No one can force us. The highest vision comes as the result of love.

There are those who believe Thomas Aquinas and Bonaventure were the two wisest men of the thirteenth century. The former was a Dominican monk, famous for both learning and piety. He had earned the title of the "Angel of the Schools." Bonaventure was the general and the chief intellectual leader of the Franciscan order. A notable legend states that once the two spent a day together in learned conversation. Before leaving, Aquinas asked to see Bonaventure's library. Bonaventure led him to his monastic cell. Opening the door he pointed to the crucifix before which he daily prayed. Quietly he said, "There it is." Power comes when one reverently looks on the cross of the Saviour.

The face of Teresa was wreathed with beauty and charming gladness. This came from her long contemplation of God. Here was a demonstration of spiritual power. It explains how she swept the world her way, building over thirty religious houses and so living that she has commanded the attention of the religious world for fourteen hundred years. That power was the result of her gaze upon the Christ. When we are wise, we lift our eyes unto the hill of Calvary, from whence cometh our help.

Here is the deeper and higher meaning of the Holy Communion. It is vitally relevant to what Paul had in mind when he said: "Whatsoever things are true, . . . honorable, . . . just, . . . pure, . . . lovely, . . . of good report; . . .

think [*logizesthe*—look with your mind, gaze] on these things!"

He meant for us so to think upon eternal things that they actually become the constant, steadfast vision of our soul. When we are wise, we keep looking upon the finest—the highest, the holiest, Christ himself!

> And so that one Face,
>   Far from vanish, rather grows;
> Or decomposes but to recompose,
>   Becomes my universe that sees and knows.

"Be Ye Doers of the Word"

ROY A. BURKHART

In the old testament there is the precious verse which says, "Ye have compassed this mountain long enough: turn ye northward." If one has encompassed the mountain of ideas and ideals, if he has come into a deep and wonderful union with God, then he must "turn northward." Then he participates in and faces life in all its reality.

In Isaiah is the verse, "They that wait upon the Lord shall renew their strength; they shall mount up with wings as eagles; they shall run, and not be weary; and they shall walk, and not faint." If we wait on the Lord, then our zeal will not flag. Then we maintain our spirit no matter what the experiences of life.

Isn't it interesting that Jesus tells us again and again that not unto him who saith, Lord, Lord, but unto him who *doeth* the will of the Father belongs the kingdom of God. When you read the Sermon on the Mount, you discover that he said, "Whosoever heareth these sayings of mine, and doeth them, I will liken him unto a wise man, which built his house upon a rock." You notice that he did not say, "Unto him who believeth, or talketh," but who *doeth*.

I once read in the headlines of a newspaper that in fifty years America will be the mightiest nation on the earth. Yes, but only if she is mighty in character, in God, in obedience to the will of God. If we hear and do, we shall be likened unto a man whose house is built upon the rock.

You remember the story of the king who forgave a man his debts; and then the man went out and threw a man who owed him into jail. Think how much we have received: the mercy, the forgiveness, the love, the grace. But how do we treat other people? Having received so much, do we pass it along? It is a real test.

When we come to take the bread, just what does it mean? The bread symbolizes all that is given. Think of all that is given to sustain our bodies, to heal them, and to help them be fit to be the temple of the Holy Spirit. Think of all that is given, for God has given us his very nature. We are his sons and daughters. Everything is available for our body's needs; everything is available for our awareness of ourselves. The secret of my identity is hidden in the love and mercy of God. But whatever is in God is really identical with him; for his infinite simplicity admits no division and no distinction. Therefore I cannot hope to find myself anywhere except in him. Ultimately the only way that I can be myself is to become identified with him in whom is hidden the reason and fulfillment of my existence. There is therefore only one problem on which all my existence, my peace, and my happiness depends: to discover myself in discovering God. If I find him, I will find myself; and if I find my true self, I will find him.

Why is it that we so rarely partake of the bread of life? If only we would eat of it, and find our full awareness, and come into a real sense of sonship and daughtership, we would be alive.

I recently received a four-page letter from a man who described to me his awakening. It was a thrilling testimony. Now and then someone does partake of the bread. He does become alive and responsive to the revelation of God, knowing his true nature which is divine. The bread is at the Communion Table not only for our bodies but for our spiritual lives as well. We can partake until we achieve union with God in his world, within ourselves, and within every man.

And the cup, what does it symbolize? It is the symbol of blood, and blood means life. During the war it hurt me very deeply that they would not accept my blood because my blood pressure was too low. I wanted to give of my blood because in doing so I knew that I would give life to men.

If we have eaten of the bread of life and received the gift of eternal life, then we can share the cup of life, be it the cup of joy, of success, of mystery, of truth unknown, or of suffering. If we are alive with real life, if we have the gift of life eternal, we can accept any cup that life offers and drink it with a song in our hearts. I have seen it again and again, and I know it is true.

And not only will we share the cup life brings to us, but also we will share the cup of others. We give to others the cup of joy, of love, of friendship. We give it in terms of thoughtfulness, of kindness, of service, of money, of every act, including our prayers for others. We do it not because we should but because we love.

If one does not believe, he does not do; if he does not do, he has not prayed. The minute we are alive with the real life of God, then we serve; we are restless to do it. Recently when with our college group at camp I saw a girl who was restless to serve others, to see that all were happy. As she poured water for the meal, I thought of him who said, "Whosoever shall give you a cup of water to drink in my name, . . . shall not lose his reward." I remember a man and woman who not long ago joined our church with great gratitude and happiness. They immediately made their pledge. Soon afterward they read a certain paragraph in the parish paper, and they sent another hundred dollars, not because they thought they should, but because they loved.

The man who wrote the letter to which I referred told me that five years ago he began to tithe, and then for him the calendar was split, and everything has been different since. There is now a joy, a peace, a satisfaction in his heart; and incidentally, greater success. Having given, he discovers that he still has.

If we eat the bread and have the life, then not only do we share the cup personally, but we see to it that every man has his cup of joy and hope and faith, and we even share the cup of suffering until it almost becomes a blessing. We do it by every possible deed, by every constructive thought, by the fullest service, by the full sharing of our money. And then when we have reached our extremity, we share it further in prayer.

When we eat the bread and share the cup in the Communion service, we may pray: "Our Father, feed us now with the bread of life and free us from anything that will keep us from partaking fully of thy grace. And grant unto us the gift of life eternal. And having received, may we share. Amen."

The New Chapter

ALFRED H. FREEMAN

THE FIRST SCENE:

The year is A.D. 67. The place is a prison in Rome. A man sits with his papyrus spread before him, his quill poised in his hand. His days are numbered. Already the shadow of the block lies before him. Soon he is to be beheaded. In this moment of meditation he sees the past as his memory presents it in kaleidoscopic review.

He relives the interesting experiences of his boyhood in Tarsus. He remembers the long sunny afternoons, many of which he spent lying on top of his house looking at the blue skies above him and wondering about the days of the future. His school days in Jerusalem pass before him, and he recalls the lifted horizons that came to him on those occasions, the growing prestige that was his among the leaders of the nation, and particularly his rapid rise to a place of leadership in the church. He thinks of that day when he was commissioned to persecute the Christians and how enthusiastically he started out toward Damascus for this purpose. Then he thinks of that glorious day on the road to Damascus when the supernatural light burst around him, and faith came into his life; for he heard Jesus speak. He remembers how his life was changed; and he lets his memory carry him down this new way, across the countries by foot and on camel back, across the lakes and seas by ships to other countries, and at long last now to a Roman prison.

His fingers caress carelessly a long scar which was left by a stone thrown in hatred. His back twitches as he recalls the lashes and the rods with which he was beaten. Long tortuous nights and hot days on storm-tossed seas as a shipwrecked traveler have left their marks upon mind and body. Now the filtered light of the sunshine comes once more through the bars of the prison cell; Paul's executioners are at the door.

He writes with feverish rapidity to his beloved friend Timothy: "I know whom I have believed, and am persuaded that he is able to keep that which I have committed unto him against that day" (II Tim. 1:12).

This he writes despite the fact that his life has not been easy. Circumstances have banded themselves together to hinder him and to thwart his dreams. He has suffered; yet out of all these experiences he has forged a faith in Almighty God, to whom he committed his very soul and every activity of his life. He believes with all his being that his God is able to keep him against the days of the future with all of their terror, with all of their suffering, even in the hour of his impending death.

Paul's faith is a confidence in God so deep that God does not have to explain his actions in order to hold the love of his child. This, as someone has said, is the highest faith possible to attain.

Weeks later, when this letter comes into the hands of Timothy, it opens for him a new chapter of his life. He knows firsthand of the trials and the suffering of his beloved father in the gospel. He too sees in retrospect all the past sufferings of Paul. He sees his beaten body as it is dragged from the city of Lystra and left for dead. He sees the frail little man as he comes from the terror of the days of shipwreck. He pictures the awful lonesomeness of that prison cell; then like a great Amen comes this testimony: "I . . . am persuaded that he is able to keep that which I have committed." Timothy's eyes fill with tears as he thinks of the depth of faith in these words from the heart of Paul. No explanation is needed from God. In simple and childlike faith he follows the pilgrimage of his long way, sure of the divine love and positive of God's divine guidance.

Timothy reads the statement again and asks himself a soul-searching question, "Am I persuaded that God is able to keep that which I have committed? Am I, Timothy, absolutely sure?" Evidently he is sure; for tradition has it that he becomes the first Bishop of Ephesus and there dies a martyr's death, still positive of God's love. Surely positive enough to be able to say the same words that his friend had written years before. "I . . . am persuaded that [God] is able to keep that which I have committed against even the hour of my death."

THE SECOND SCENE:

The time is a few years ago in our own country. The place is a small village. The people that make up the village are very like the people who go to make up the city in which we live today. Some of them are devoutly religious; some are extremely careless. Some are positive of God's guidance in their daily lives; some are trying to put off their decisions as to how they would live with God. And some are just living as if God didn't matter at all—as if he did not exist.

In that little town there lives a village blacksmith whose name is John. He prides himself on the fact that he is an infidel. He curses the Church and all the things that it stands for and the lessons that it teaches. He laughs at the idea of God. Because of this he is called by the villagers "Devil John." They leave him alone.

The scene opens two miles out in the country, where an elderly man and his wife are engaged in their nightly devotions. Again they are reading from the old letter of Paul to his friend Timothy. "I know whom I have believed, and am persuaded that he is able to keep that which I have committed unto him against that day." The book is placed back upon the table, and the couple go to their well-earned rest.

At the first break of day the old man arises and says: "Molly, hurry! Get breakfast ready. I have to go to town and see Devil John."

Quickly he eats, gets out his old overcoat, buckles on his overshoes, and hitches his horse to the buggy. Through the raw, misty weather he rides over the snow. He arrives at the blacksmith shop just as John is kindling the fire in the forge.

"What brings you to town so early; do you need some work today?"

The old man drags a nail keg near the fire and replies: "John, I want to tell you a story. I dreamed that I died last night and went to heaven. It was far more beautiful than I had ever imagined. The saints were there. Peter, James, John, and Paul. The saintly people of our own home town were there, old Mr. Thomas and Mrs. Brown who lived in the big house. What joy we had talking together. The days went rapidly by; months grew into years before I was aware of it. I began to notice that as the angels went from that holy place into this world, they returned, bringing others of our friends to this beautiful place. Dr. McClellan and Molly, whom I loved all these years, arrived. Happiness was there. Then I noticed I was looking for someone. I discovered it was you I was missing. I asked the angels as they returned time and time again. 'Why doesn't John come?' They did not know. At last I went to him whom we called the master, and I said: 'Tell me, Lord, why doesn't John come?'

"The Lord's countenance clouded with sorrow. He said, 'No one ever asked him.'

"John, I am asking you now. Aren't you persuaded that he is able to keep that life that you can commit unto him against that day?"

John, looking into the earnest face of his friend, is suddenly persuaded that God *can* keep his life. For John there begins a new chapter in his life: faith, that needs no explanation from the great, good God, to hold his love.

THE THIRD SCENE:

The year is now; the place my church. It is beautifully lighted by the sunshine of God's goodness. After nineteen hundred years I read again the letter of Paul to Timothy. "I . . . am persuaded that he is able to keep that which I have committed unto him against that day." We record our faith in his ability to keep us against the day of judgment by the celebration of the Holy Communion, central scrament of the Christian Church. As the sacrament of baptism marks our entrance into the Christian life, so the sacrament of the Holy Communion is the evidence of our continuation in his way.

The Holy Communion is not to be treated as though it were just another church service. It should be of eternal significance deep down inside our hearts. It should be a new chapter in our spiritual lives. Remember the challenge of the general invitation to the supper of our Lord: "Ye that do truly and earnestly repent of your sins . . . " Are we willing to do that? Are we ashamed of our sins, our secret sins, our sins of indifference, sins of thought, word, and deed? We should come to the Communion Table, in the spirit of repentance, saying, "We do earnestly repent and are heartily sorry for these our misdoings." Let no one come with an unconfessed sin.

"And are in love and charity with your neighbors . . . " This is no time to argue about who our neighbors are. They are the sons and daughters of God everywhere. All are made in his image; all have a capacity for divine fellowship. We should come to the Communion Table but leave our prejudices, our superiority complexes, our racial bitternesses behind; come with hearts filled with love for all men, even as God "so loved the world"; kneel at the table, at least in spirit, with all races and conditions of men everywhere and as brothers say, "Our Father."

"And intend to lead a new life, following the commandments of God . . . " Christ pleads for our proposal to lead a new life, to write a new chapter, to commit our all to him. Let us say again in the words of Paul, " I . . . am persuaded that he is able to keep that [life] which I have committed unto him against that day." "Are ye able?" May we say, "Lord, we are able"?

The Cross as Contemporary

SAMUEL McCREA CAVERT

There they crucified him.—Luke 23:33

IN ONE OF THE MOVING NEGRO SPIRITUALS THERE IS A haunting refrain, "Were you there when they crucified my Lord?" The answer which every sensitive Christian who understands the meaning of the cross must make is, "Yes, I was there."

For the sins which once sent Jesus to Calvary are the same sins which we find in our own hearts today. The motives of the Pharisees and of the Sadducees, of Judas and Pilate, as we read of them in the Gospels, were the same kind of motives which animate us. Their attitudes are our attitudes also.

The Pharisees were the "good people" of Jerusalem, a respectable and respected group, scrupulous in observing the Ten Commandments and all the requirements of the moral law. They were the Puritans of their time. The trouble with them was not that they were unconcerned with religion and morality but that they were too narrow in both their religion and their morals. While keeping up all the conventional standards they were neglecting the weightier matters of justice and right which were the great concerns of Jesus. So the Pharisees were there when they crucified the Lord. And in the Pharisee I discover a man very much like myself.

The Sadducees were the priestly class, the professional representatives of religion, those who supervised the temple ceremonies. They were the people who held the comfortable places in the ecclesiastical system. They maintained all the conservative traditions. The trouble with them was not that they were bad but that they would not tolerate anything which might have an adverse effect on their own status and position. So the Sadducees were there when they crucified the Lord. And in the Sadducee, again, I discover a man very much like myself.

Even Judas and Pilate, the two individuals who played the principal roles in the Crucifixion, were not depraved and despicable men. Judas had enough decent impulses to lead him to be at least a halfhearted follower of the Master for a time. Apparently it was an overdeveloped case of self-concern which at last got the better of him. He could not resist the temptation of easy money. Perhaps, too, as is hinted in the motion picture "The King of Kings," he was ambitious for power in the kingdom which Jesus was to establish, and betrayed the cause when he found that in that kingdom there would be no one sitting on the right hand or the left. For Judas the first question always was, "What is there in it for me?" So Judas was there when they crucified the Lord. And I discover all too much of Judas in myself.

Pilate, likewise, was no ruthless and brutal figure. He was the representative of government, and in this capacity his one concern was to maintain law and order. He was not going to let things get out of hand because of the revolutionary teaching of a young idealist. But he seems to have been a man of good personal character. He was honest enough to say, after examining Jesus, "I find no fault in him," and tentatively suggested that the prisoner might be discharged. But when he saw how unpoular this decision would be, he changed his mind. He did not have enough moral stamina to stand up aganist an overwhelming majority. He was a timid compromiser, always ready to fall in line. So Pilate was there when they crucified the Lord. And I discover all too much of Pilate in myself.

There was one other factor that contributed to the crucifixion of Jesus, the crowd that passed by or looked on, thoughtless and careless. Their part was only a passive one. They cast no vote against him. They drove no nails into his hands. But they could have saved him, and they let him die. They were neutral at a critical hour when a man of conviction and integrity would have stood up and been counted. They were more interested in Barabbas, a bitter nationalist who hated the Romans, than in one who insisted that love is the saving force in life. The trouble with them was not that they were hostile to Jesus but simply that they were apathetic and irresolute. So the fickle and easygoing crowd was not without responsibility for what happened. And in that crowd around the cross we see ourselves. We were there when they crucified the Lord.

All this makes it clear that the Crucifixion was not the result of some enormous conspiracy of evil. It came about because men were too selfish to think beyond their own private interests, too insensitive to understand the spiritual issues that were at stake, too indifferent to devote themselves to high and challenging ends. The crucifixion of Jesus came to pass not because there were certain men who were outrageously wicked but because there were so many who were just about as good as we are—and no better.

In the light of this truth we see that the cross of Christ is intensely contemporary. The scene on Calvary is not merely an isolated incident that happened nineteen hundred years ago. It is really an epitome of human history through-out the centuries. The most terrible thing that can be said about the world in which we live is that it is always the kind of place in which Jesus is crucified.

A deeper reason why the Cross is always contemporary is that it reveals not merely our human attitudes toward the crucified Christ but also—and far more important—God's attitude toward man. The Cross manifests, in a way that transcends any particular age, God's suffering for our sinful world. To mature Christian thought the death of Jesus is not simply that of a martyr in Palestine under the Roman empire. It is the unique disclosure of the redemptive love that is the ultimate reality in the universe. If God were like an unmoved monarch on a throne, men would rightly hate him. How could they love one who remained aloof from a world of suffering in which he did not himself share? But if God is what Jesus on the cross shows him to be, then our souls can find peace in our suffering and courage for our struggle. Then we can understand the force of G. A. Studdert-Kennedy's lines:

Peace does not mean the end of all our striving,
    Joy does not mean the drying of our tears;
Peace is the power that comes to souls arriving
    Up to the light where God Himself appears.

Bread of Thy Body give me for my fighting,
    Give me to drink Thy Sacred Blood for wine,
While there are wrongs that need me for the righting,
    While there is warfare splendid and divine.

Give me, for light, the sunshine of Thy sorrow,
    Give me, for shelter, shadow of Thy Cross,

Give me to share the glory of Thy morrow,
Gone from my heart the bitterness of Loss.[1]

Another truth which emphasizes the contemporary character of the Cross is that the Cross is not for Christ alone
but for the Christian also. Our Lord made that completely
clear: "If any man will come after me, let him deny himself,
and take up his cross." One of his great interpreters summed
it all up when he said, "Hereby know we love, because he
laid down his life for us: and we ought to lay down our lives
for the brethren" (I John 3:16 A.S.V.).

In one sense what Christ did was done once for all: he
revealed God's love so completely that his cross is the great
redeeming force in history. But there is also a sense in which
we have to carry on what Christ began. He is not to bear the
Cross alone and all the world go free. To the degree that we
are really Christian we reflect something, at least, of the
meaning of the Cross in our own lives. What the spirit of
the Cross may mean for an ordinary man today may be
gloriously illustrated by another reference to Studdert-
Kennedy. When he was in the trenches in the First World
War, he wrote a letter to his little son at home. These were
his words—words that are windows disclosing the inner
life of a true follower of the Christ of the Cross:

The first prayer I want my son to learn to say for me is not,
"God, keep Daddy safe," but "God, make Daddy brave, and if
he has hard things to do make him strong to do them." Life
and death don't matter much, my son, but right and wrong do.
. . . I suppose you'd like to put into your prayer a bit about my
safety, too—and Mother would. Well, put it in, but *afterwards*,
always afterwards, because it does not matter near so much.

[1] "The Suffering God" from *The Unutterable Beauty*, copyright 1936
by Harper & Bros., and Hodder & Stoughton, Ltd., London.

I Will Pray

WILLIAM L. STIDGER

Evening, and morning, and at noon, will I pray, and cry aloud: and he shall hear my voice.—Ps. 55:17

COMMUNION MEANS MEDITATION, INTROSPECTION, REpentance, renewal of spiritual power; in a word, prayer. It may mean other things historically and from a ritualistic viewpoint. But to the everyday church worshiper it means an attitude of devotion, meditation, and prayer.

To me one of the most beautiful lines in the whole biblical literature is "I will meditate on thee in the night watches." I merely wish to extend that spirit of meditation which comes with the Communion service into praying at evening, morning, and noon, conscious that my God and Father will hear my prayer.

Several years ago when I was on a daily nationwide hookup for N.B.C. in New York City, I was presenting a Communion hour to and for my radio listeners, and in seeking a theme I found this one, "I will pray!"

But when I began to search for a hymn to go with it, I could not find what I wanted; so I sat down and wrote one for that special broadcast, and Dr. James Houghton, my director of music on that broadcast, adapted it to music, the melody of a great Mozart hymn which is already in the hymnology of the Church. Here is the hymn, based on our text:

I will pray when morning glory
   Gilds the eastern hills with gold,
When the dew has washed the tulip,
   And dawn's tale of time is told.
I will kneel before Thine altars
   And burn incense at Thy shrines;
Incense of the rose and lilac,
   Locust-bloom and wind-washed pines.

I will pray at noon, dear Master,
   When all life is high with hope
And the sun has halved the circle
   In its mighty sweep and scope;
When life's blood is coursing wildly
   In a full majestic stream,
When the tide of strength is running
   To its daring flow and dream.

I will pray, dear God, when darkness
   Throws its vesper shadows 'round;
In the silence I will listen,
   Kneeling on Thy Holy Ground.
I will meet Thy tryst at twilight
   When the silent shadows sleep
And all birds, and beasts, and children
   Into dreamland softly creep.

What I am trying to say through this text and this hymn is that "I will meditate on thee" not only "in the night watches" but "evening, and morning, and at noon, will I pray, and cry aloud: and he shall hear my voice." The Communion ritual is for childhood, for youth, and for old age.

Recently I had the exciting adventure of taking my three grandchildren to their first Communion. Their parents had felt that they were too young to understand what Communion meant. Those grandchildren were then six, seven, and ten years of age; and I felt that they ought to be exposed to this quiet, beautiful, reverent spiritual experience of Communion. I knew that it could do them no harm and that the pageantry of it, the beauty of it, the memory of it, would mark a spiritual milestone in their lives.

Before we went to that first Communion, I told them the story of Jesus and little children—of how the mothers brought their children to Jesus one day on a Judean hillside and how the disciples rebuked them, and how Jesus said, "Suffer the little children to come unto me, and forbid them not: for of such is the kingdom of God."

I told the children of the Annunciation, of the coming of the Christ child, and of how "his mother kept all these sayings in her heart." I recalled to their minds the story of the birth of that child, of the three Wise Men, of the disciples, of the baby in the manger. Their eyes brightened over those familiar stories. Then I brought them down to the day when Jesus took little children and blessed them, and to add to the spiritual romance and beauty of that scene I quoted to them Joaquin Miller's poem describing that event:

> Then reaching His hands, He said, lowly:
>   "Of such is my Kingdom" and then
> Took the little brown babes in the Holy
>   White hands of the Savior of men;
> Held them up to his heart and caressed them,
>   Put His cheeks down to theirs as in prayer;
> Held them close to his cheeks, and so, blessed them
>   With baby hands hid in His hair.[1]

[1]Used by permission of Juanita Joaquina Miller.

They were deeply impressed with the poetic interpretation of that divine event of Jesus blessing little children and asked to have it read to them severeal times.

In that mood I took them to their first Communion; led them gently by the hands, knelt with them at the altar, and partook with them of the sacred bread and wine; stayed a moment for meditation, and walked back to our seats.

Those three children, Heather, Billy, and Jacky, were profoundly impressed with that experience. They sat quietly through all the rest of that church service and watched the others walk quietly up to the altar, and when it was all over we went home with hushed hearts.

Neither their parents nor I have ever heard the last of that Communion service. On the way home Jacky, the ten-year-old, said, "I like that church, and I like what we did. Let's do it again sometime."

I shall never forget what Luther Burbank, the great naturalist, said to me about the spiritual sensitiveness of a little child's soul, "A child's soul has a seismographic sensitiveness to spiritual things." Then he went on to expand that idea by saying:

I have noticed in my experimental work that metals have the least responsiveness to outside influences. It takes terrific heat, acids, and pressures to change metals. The next most sensitive thing is a growing, living plant. They respond to outside influences much quicker than metals. I will not even allow a man who drinks or smokes to work with my plants, for even the breath of an alcoholic affects the sensitive plants. However, the most sensitive plant of all is a little child. A child will respond to the slightest outside suggestion, story, sermon, idea, love, and affection. Children respond to pictures, music, suggestions. A child is the most sensitive plant on earth, and an adult can make what he wishes out of the soul of a little child.

That is what I mean by exposing a child to the spiritual influence of the Communion service as early as that child can walk and talk, and feel and think. "Evening, and morning, and at noon, will I pray, and cry aloud: and he shall hear my voice."

> I will pray at noon, dear Master,
> When all life is high with hope.

In this couplet we see that Communion, meditation, and prayer ought to be the experience of youth as well as childhood. The attitude of reverence, prayer, and spiritual communion ought to be the regular and habitual experience of young people.

> When life's blood is coursing wildly
> In a full majestic stream,
> When the tide of strength is running
> To its daring flow and dream.

In the Abbey paintings of the Holy Grail which have long been a favorite haunt of tourists to Boston, there is one beautiful panel called "The Vigil" in which young Sir Galahad kneels at the altar of the Church of God before he goes out on the long and hazardous quest for the Holy Grail. In preparation for that task, in the full flush of his youth, he feels it worth while to have communion with his God, to "meditate on [him] in the night watches," to pray in preparation for that great and sacred journey. That, the authorities tell me, is the most popular panel of all the series of murals and the one which college youth always buy in post card form to send to parents and friends.

Youth always responds to real spiritual suggestion, for youth is a time of dreams, idealism, and spiritual possibilities. I am always impressed when I myself go into the

Boston Library to look at these Sir Abbey paintings to find a group of young college students around that panel of "The Vigil," watching it with reverence. For them that experience is sort of a communion with the high and holy things, things to which the untrammeled soul of youth responds. On that fact I believe that parents, teachers, and preachers can always count. It is our duty and our privilege to see to it that the youth of our day are exposed to the beautiful experience of communion and meditation as often as possible. There may be a certain shyness in youth about walking up to the altar of the church to partake of the Holy Communion; but if parents unobstrusively, gently, kindly, and tenderly go with them from childhood on, it will become a spiritual habit. It will bring its spiritual harvest of beauty and reverence, the memory of which will never die. "Evening, and morning, and at noon, will I pray, and cry aloud: and he shall hear my voice."

Childhood, youth, and age need the spiritual refreshment, the tender introspection, the quiet meditation of the Communion experience. The seismographic sensitiveness of childhood, the rugged self-confidence, and the self-sufficient period of youth need and respond to the spiritual simplicities and sincere idealism of the Communion ritual. The periods of adulthood and old age likewise need this experience.

Life presses in on us, beats us down. Life with all its turbulency, tumult, and its tempestuous seas tosses us about until we are utterly confused, often broken in spirit and defeated. Dr. Parkhurst, the great New York preacher of a generation ago, once said, "As I grow older, I find that I preach more and more to broken hearts." When asked why, he said:

Because in adulthood and old age we ultimately discover that we are failures, that we are not going to set the world on fire, to make a conquest of all events. We are business failures; our ideal dreams of youth have been dissipated; we find that we are just ordinary people after all. Ninety per cent of the people with whom I deal and to whom I preach are brokenhearted people in one way or another. That is why I say that as I grow older I preach more to broken hearts.

It is to the defeated, the downcast, the failure, the broken-hearted, that the Communion comes with its sacred and blessed comfort and confidence. It is to him that the table of our blessed Lord and Saviour brings a panacea and a spiritual healing. It is literally a "Communion" with him who instituted that Last Supper in his time of trial, defeat, and tragedy.

For be it remembered that Jesus had a wistful hunger in his lonely heart on that eventful night. He sought fellowship with his beloved disciples when he knew what was ahead for him; what tragedy, heartache, and heartbreak faced him. It was in his moment of defeat and tragedy that he requested his disciples to prepare a place for the Communion as we call it in the Church today, a Hebrew custom, a family gathering, a spiritual preparation.

In the Hebrew tradition the ritual which we call Communion was used to celebrate any crisis in the Hebrew family life: marriage, the event of a long journey on the part of the Hebrew family, a business venture, illness, disaster, trouble in the family. Then it was that the elder brother of the Hebrew family or the father called the family together for that sacred family gathering. It was a sacred ritual then, and it is still a sacred ritual in the modern Church. It is a re-membering. "This do in remembrance of me," said Christ to his bewildered disciples.

Yes, Communion is prayer, introspection, penitence, worship; and more: It is a remembering. And perhaps that is its most important psychological and spiritual function. At least Jesus seemed to think so, for he emphasized that to his disciples. "And when they had sung an hymn, they went out into the mount of Olives."

I have a confrere in the Boston University School of Theology, Dr. Richard Cameron. He built a beautiful home fifteen years ago in historic Concord, Massachusetts. When he and his wife talked with the architect, they told him that they wanted designed in the basement of that home, in addition to the usual "rumpus room" in which the children could romp and play, a little gothic chapel in which the children could pray. That architect, being an idealist, liked that suggestion and designed a beautiful, small gothic room with an altar and the sacred symbols of worship. From the beginning each of the five little tots who came into that home was taken into that sacred cloister for daily worship and once a month for Communion. It became as natural to those children to worship God in that small chapel as it was to play boisterous childhood games in the adjoining rumpus room. They grew up with that expectation, that experience, and that family ritual. The Communion was as eagerly looked forward to as a party or a picnic. It was done with great reverence and spiritual beauty. Poems were read; the scriptures describing the original Communion were always a part of that service. Each child partook of that Communion with quiet sincerity and respect.

I spoke with those wise parents early in that experience after the new home had been consecrated with prayer in the little chapel and asked them why they had included that chapel in their plans. Dr. Cameron replied: "So that my children will have a memory of Communion and worship in their own home under reverent conditions. No matter what happens to them in later life, they will remember Christ's command, 'This do in remembrance of me.' "

The years have passed; those children have grown up and finished college; some of them are married. Recently when I was talking with one of them we happened to mention the little chapel where the family Communion was conducted, and that son said: "The most beautiful memory of my childhood is the Communion services in our little home chapel when Father would say as he gave us the wafer and wine, 'This do in remembrance of me.' "

"Evening, and morning, and at noon, will I pray and cry aloud: and he shall hear my voice."

Save Your High Moments

ROY L. SMITH

Master, it is good for us to be here: and let us make
three tabernacles; one for thee, and one for Moses, and
one for Elijah.   —Luke 9:33

Peter, with his brother Andrew, was the head of a
prosperous Capernaum fishing firm which operated a fleet
of vessels on the Sea of Galilee. He was a fascinating personality, one of those rare individuals who gravitate to positions
of leadership by the sheer force of character. A bit inclined
to impetuosity, which was a part of his strength, he was
aggressive, adroit, and capable of a persistent and passionate
devotion. His name appears in the New Testament more
frequently than that of any other except that of Jesus.
He seems to have been a man that was built in only two
gears, high speed forward and reverse.

The situation had been growing increasingly worse for
Jesus over a period of several months prior to the time of
our story. Almost anything might happen if he went down
to the Passover in Jerusalem. A single incident, insignificant
in itself, might become the occasion for some high tragedy.
Because this situation weighed heavily on the mind of the
Master, he betook himself to a mountain to spend the
night in prayer. Since he seemed to find strength in the
companionship of three of his disciples, Peter, James, and
John, he took them along.

Exactly what transpired that night in the exalted rendezvous with God no one will ever know. Jesus had been praying for some time when the disciples discovered that from him there emanated a strange radiance. They spoke of it years afterward; how his face shone and his garments glistened. They knew that an altogether unprecedented event was taking place before their very eyes.

Just when they were awed into silence, two celestial figures appeared, Moses, the founder of the nation, and Elijah, the forerunner of the prophets. And the three of them talked of the death that was awaiting Jesus at Jerusalem. Never in all human experience had human eyes rested on such a scene, nor had human ears heard such words as were spoken. The three fish dealers had been given the greatest insight into the mind of heaven that had ever been revealed to man. Peter was shaken to the depth of his being. Soon the heavenly visitors took their leave and left Jesus only, standing on the mountain with his three disciples. When he was able to speak, Peter said, "Master, it is good for us to be here: and let us make three tabernacles; one for thee, and one for Moses, and one for Elijah."

Perhaps it was not a wise suggestion which Peter made. Mountaintops are hard to reach, and tabernacles built on them are likely to be neglected. But the apostle was so stirred by what had transpired that he was trying to perpetuate his high moment, save it, preserve it for the day when he would be in desperate need of it.

Life for most of us moves along in a rather monotonous level. We arise about the same time every morning, eat about the same breakfast, hurry off to the same work, follow the same routine, indulge in the same small talk, and get excited about the same things every day. As one dear old lady described the situation, "the trouble with life is that it is so daily."

Occasionally, however, there comes a rare and luminous moment which is unlike any other hour we have ever spent. Under the inspiration of such a transfiguration we think things we never thought before; we dream dreams we never dreamed before; we believe ourselves capable of achievements which normally we would think fantastic. In the midst of those high moments it is easy to believe in God. It is as though we can reach out and touch the hem of Christ's garment—as though heaven were all about us.

Different people experience these high moments under different circumstances. A young bank clerk whose ears were cluttered with the clicking of adding machines all day long experienced such a high moment when he heard a great choir sing Handel's "Hallelujah Chorus." A boy from the backwoods, his soul starved for beauty, experienced such a high moment the first time he stood before a great picture in an art museum. A young preacher experienced such a high moment one morning in a hospital when he held in his arms for the first time his own first-born. In that moment he settled more questions about the fatherhood of God than throughout his entire seminary studies.

It is in these high moments that we meet God; we hear him speak; we feel the pressure of his spirit upon our lives. And the great problem of life is *how to save these high moments* and make them permanent. Daguerre, the famous French scientist, said to be the father of modern photography, became convinced that an image could be captured on a sensitized plate and made permanent. With this in mind he coated a thin sheet of tin with a chemical emulsion and exposed it to light under controlled conditions. But nothing happened. Undaunted, he tried another emulsion, then another, and another. At last one day with a new emulsion he dropped the thin plate in a crude camera, and when it was removed from the camera, the image lingered. He had caught the image with the sensitive plate. All he had to do then was to make the image permanent.

The apostle Paul toward the close of his career told some of his friends that he had caught a glimpse of the Christ. It was on the road to Damascus that Paul saw God through Christ, and that one experience changed his entire life. He did not need to be stricken blind a second or a third time. Once was enough. That amazing vision he made permanent in his life. He held the image ever before him. This explains his great devotion. The spiritually successful are those who have made their temporary transfigurations permanent. They have saved their high moments.

There have come to all of us enough high moments to redeem us if we but conserve them. The trouble is we allow them to grow dim or to disappear. We fall short of our dreams and begin to doubt them. We struggle and go down under the flood and become cynical. We share in the shameful and excuse ourselves on the pretext that "we are only human, you know," as if to be human meant to be low and lewd. We forget that the prodigal son on his way back to his father's house was just as human as he was on his way out to the far country.

I once knew a man who was one of the most important business leaders of his community. Respected for his ability and with a magnetic personality, he was given the most responsible tasks of his community. But he was lewd and vulgar in his speech. At a committee meeting around a lunch table he confided to the minister who sat beside him. "Doctor," he said, "I don't suppose you will believe it, but I studied for the ministry at one time. In fact I preached a little during my sophomore year. Sounds silly, doesn't it? Think of me being a preacher."

"No, John," said the clergyman. "it doesn't sound silly. It sounds wonderful. Tell me, John, what would you give to be able to go back to those days and be the man you were then, think the thoughts you thought then, dream the dreams you dreamed then, live on the high level where you lived then? Weren't those about the most wonderful years of your life? Have you ever known anything so splendid since?"

There was a moment of silence as the businessman dropped his head. At last he looked up, sober and earnest now. "You are right, preacher. They were my best years. I have been losing ground ever since. I would give everything I have for a return of those years of high aspiration." He had lost his high moments.

The first thing a man must do to save his high moments is to hold them in high respect. A reporter for a great Chicago newspaper had an interview with Gipsy Smith, the famous evangelist. Something in the interview recalled to the evangelist the occasion when two hundred girls from the red-light district had invaded his meeting. As memory cast its spell over the old evangelist, he detailed the appeal he made to these girls that they might forsake their sins and accept the forgiveness of a loving Christ.

It was all so natural, so unplanned, and so simple that the interviewer forgot that he had come for a story. He seemed to feel himself following the sinners down to an altar of repentance. A tightening gathered in his throat, a mistiness suffused in his eyes, and he was almost at the point of crying out with the Philippian jailer, "What must I do to be saved?" when he suddenly remembered. He was a reporter, not a penitent. He must not let this thing get him. He had a deadline to meet.

Thrusting his best self down in the muck and the mire and scribbling hurriedly to compose his mind, he snatched up some of the glowing sentences of the evangelist and hurried back to the office. In the story that appeared was this sentence, "Ten minutes more, and he would have had me." Think of it. He managed to escape a great spiritual experience by ten minutes. He refused to hold his greatest moment in high respect!

A second suggestion must be made to one who wishes to save his high moments. Let him return, either actually or in imagination, to the scene of that transfiguration.

It was 8 A.M. on a Monday morning, and an appointment had brought the preacher down to his office earlier than usual. As he entered the sanctuary he saw a young man leaving the altar. "Hello, Bill. What are you doing here at this hour?"

The young man falteringly said, "Doctor, I have lost something, and I was looking for it."

It had been nearly six years before that this young man's mother had told the minister that she was praying that her son would be a preacher. After some months, in the midst of a Holy Communion service, this young man had knelt at the altar, and, as he took the sacred symbols of bread and wine, he breathed a simple prayer that changed the course of his life. "Lord Christ, take my life and use all of it for your kingdom's sake."

After graduating from college and three years in the seminary he was assigned to his first church. He had been there for six months when, on this morning, he returned to the church of his youth and said to the preacher, "I have lost something. I was looking for it."

"What did you lose, Bill?" asked the older churchman.

"I lost my ministry," replied the youth. "Things have been going pretty badly on my work. I had trouble with two laymen; one of my women's organizations gave me some sleepless nights; and things came to a crisis last Sunday morning. I lost my temper and exploded in the pulpit. I apologized, but it didn't help. I started to hand in my resignation to the bishop and quit the church when I decided to come here instead. I got up at 5 A.M., drove sixty miles, came into the sanctuary, and found the identical spot where I knelt six years ago. I prayed again the prayer I prayed when I entered the ministry. I wanted to see God as I saw him that morning."

"What happened?" asked the older minister.

"He came back," the youth replied, his eyes swimming in tears. "And I'm back in the ministry again. I found what I lost."

And that which the young minister experienced we all can experience. It may be impossible for us to retrace our steps over the identical trail. The church may have been torn down; the chancel may have been changed from what it was then. But we can go back over the same spiritual path. And of one thing we may be sure. God will come back to meet us there. He will show again his face to his seeking children.

Save your high moments. If ever you needed to see clearly the face of God, you need it now.

How to Be Happy

GERALD KENNEDY

Blessed are those.—Matt. 5:4 (R.S.V.)

THE SERMON ON THE MOUNT HAS BEEN THE SUBJECT OF much discussion and endless debate. The truth is that it troubles us, and we are hard put to decide just how we ought to take it. Some have argued that Jesus considered the end of the world so near that he meant this teaching for a short time only. If he had known that Christians were to live in the world for many centuries, these critics maintain, he never would have suggested such impossibly high ethics. Others have said that the sermon is addressed to the saints alone and has no general significance.

With neither of these views do I find myself in complete agreement. The Sermon on the Mount, it seems to me, is to be taken by everyone as the way of life for every man under all conditions. Jesus is giving us his insights into the ultimate meanings of life. This path does not promise that a man will make a million dollars by following it, but it does promise what the Gospel of John calls "eternal life." This is the Christian understanding of how a man may live in harmony with God's laws.

It is not likely that this sermon was preached all at one time. Matthew has probably edited the material and brought it together. Jesus said these things on different occasions and at different times. But we have here the heart of his message.

So magnificent is it that men of other religions have been influenced by it. In his book *Lead Kindly Light*, Vincent Sheean quotes Gandhi as saying, "I must warn you that my interpretation of the Gita (sacred book of Hinduism) has been criticized by orthodox scholars as being unduly influenced by the Sermon on the Mount." It would not be too much to say that no document has influenced Western civilization as much as this brief writing of less than two thousand words. It has unity and completeness. Like few other writings it carries its own authority and shines in its own light. If once we can help each other to grasp, even dimly, its greatness, it will become the subject for a lifetime of study, and it can easily be the most influential reading experience we have ever had.

Robert Sherwood in his book *Roosevelt and Hopkins* says that when President Roosevelt and Prime Minister Churchill were having a conference together during the war, they wandered far afield into history. Harry Hopkins, who was also present, rather brusquely brought them back to the subject in hand. Churchill said that after the war was over His Majesty's government was going to bestow a noble title on Hopkins. "We have already selected the title," he said. "You are to be named 'Lord Root of the Matter.'" The Sermon on the Mount is Jesus' word concerning the root of the matter in regard to life. Here we are standing on the foundations. Here are the ultimate principles to follow if we are to live as sons of God and brothers of our Lord.

For one thing Jesus is saying that happiness does not depend on comfort. He talks about the persecuted, the mourners, the poor in spirit, and calls them "blessed." It is amazing when we note how much of our effort is directed toward making ourselves comfortable. An urban civilization tends to produce too many citizens who desire a steam-heated flat and no exercise. We spend too much time in surrounding ourselves with protection against anything that disturbs our selfishness. A gadget civilization can hardly escape this cheap and trivial purpose. We seem bent on spending our best brains to produce new ways of saving ourselves from effort or pain. Finally we accept as the legitimate goal of the whole business, the production of comfort.

Success in our time is often little more than achieving money enough or power enough to get others to bear our burdens for us. We free ourselves from any labor in connection with heating our homes, and we have cars to take us everywhere. All that they demand of us is a slight pressure on the gas throttle and the brake. We no longer have to shift the gears. All this gives us leisure which has been regarded as the solution of most of our problems. Life to many a young person seems to have become a matter of insulating oneself against all mental, physical, and spiritual discomforts.

This has not worked too well. We are disillusioned with the end product, which is so often an unbearable boredom. Yet like dope addicts we plunge further and further into our despair. Our religion, which threatens to disturb us with its trumpet call, is transformed into a heresy which makes a tranquil spirit the final purpose. We are afraid to look at ourselves through the eyes of Jesus. We are afraid because we know we ought to have higher aims, and we ought to be doing more heroic things. Both Christianity and democracy stand on the faith that men will expose themselves to danger and to suffering for worthy causes. They stand or fall on the idea that men will care. They are not possible when a society prefers comfort to duty. Sacrifice is the price we have to pay for freedom.

Remember the war! Tired, bored, oversophisticated people became alive again because they were needed and much was at stake. Long hours and a myriad of discomforts were taken in stride. Out of our mourning there was born a hunger and thirst for something better. We felt sympathy with one another, and we shared each other's woes. We lived. We should have learned that comfort is not enough. We should have learned the truth of Disraeli's statement. "The European talks of progress because by the aid of a few scientific discoveries he has established a society which has mistaken comfort for civilization."

In the second place Jesus is saying that happiness does not depend on possessions. In all the Beatitudes there is not a single word about ownership, which is a radical teaching indeed. The vast majority of Americans are convinced that their unhappiness is due to a lack of goods. Hardly a man but does not believe that if he could have the luxuries which his richer neighbors have, he would be satisfied. The rest of the world feels that if it could have the wealth of America, all would be well. Jesus says nothing about things, but discusses the qualities of the heart and attitudes of the mind.

Jesus said that "man's life does not consist in the abundance of his possessions." (Luke 12:15 R.S.V.). We think it does. Jesus told of a man whose land brought forth so plentifully that he had nowhere to store his crops. He said he would tear down his old barns and build larger ones, but he would neglect his soul. "But God said to him, 'Fool! This night your soul is required of you; and the things you have prepared, whose will they be?'" (Luke 12:20-21 R.S.V.) We would regard such a man as a successful grain speculator and the flower of our society. Yet the burden of ownership and the worship of possessions destroy the quali-

ties of sensitiveness, sympathy, purity, and meekness. We
have to decide which is first and which is most important.
Jesus is saying that nothing is worth while that damages the
soul.

The most anxious people are those whose treasures can be
stolen. They are the well-to-do who are afraid that a shift in
political power will damage their investments. They are
those who are frightened that a more equitable distribution
will rob them of their possessions. They are fearful lest an
economic reversal will cut down their profits. For such as
these there is no peace, and there is no blessedness. Some
men are made great by adversity, but those whose lives are
centered in things are destroyed. They are the suicides and
the invalids which every depression produces. For it must
always follow that if a man's chief treasure is some materialistic thing he is forever at the mercy of physical forces.
He can know no peace of mind, and his freedom is so
limited as to be hardly worth mentioning.

How different is the religious person. In the Old Testament it is written, "The righteous will not be dispossessed
in hard times" (Ps. 37:19, Elmer Leslie's translation).
When men have learned to prefer being to owning, they
have freed themselves from external circumstances. Because
they are humble, they cannot be hurt. Because they have
centered their hearts on God, persecution for his sake is
a kind of joy. The right kind of person is the master of
things.

There is an old Scandinavian proverb to the effect that
the north wind made the Vikings. Jesus would say that it
is much more blessed to be a Viking than to own a yacht.
The spirit of the man is the thing which determines his
happiness or lack of it. The wrong kind of man can never
be happy with all the possessions in the world. But the right

kind of man is happy without any of the possessions of the world. I have a friend who is one of those wise simpletons; he is at the same time the joy and despair of his friends. He never can stay on the subject or go directly to the point, yet if one has the patience, he often says something important. In the midst of a rather wandering conversation this friend said to me one day, "It's tough to be weak after having fallen into a spotlight." He meant, I suppose, that if one can keep his own inadequacy hidden, it is bearable. But when life suddenly puts a spotlight on us and reveals our weakness and spiritual poverty for all to see, that is the crowning shame. And life is always doing that. When that time comes, all our possessions are embarrassments. We know that what we are is the decisive thing.

Finally Jesus is saying that happiness depends on the right desires. We go wrong when we assume that life is simply a matter of winning control over lawless passions by our spirit which is always good. Not so! It is our spirit which is so often bad. We have to recognize that our whole rational drive may be wrong. This is what our fathers called original sin, and whatever we may call it, the experience is as real today as it was then.

In our time we have assumed that anybody's idea of the good life is as valid as any other. We only have to set our goals and then accomplish them to be happy. Nonsense! If we set out for the wrong goals, the very accomplishment of them is the worst thing that can happen to us. If the Lord always gave us what we think we want, we would be in trouble most of the time. Some things cost too much. Thoreau once remarked that he measured everything by the amount of life he had to pay for it. People are paying too much for some very shoddy products. Some things wear out too soon. We pay a big price for something that fades at the end of the day. Young people risk everything for a thrill or for lust. It is soon over, but the price has to be paid for years.

This is all a problem of the heart. Jesus was always going under the surface. He determined first of all what kind of creatures we are, and then he spoke to the very center of our beings. When our desires have been purified, then we can trust them, and they will lead us to our heart's desire. We have to trust Jesus and let him teach us to desire the right things. He is doing that for us in the Sermon on the Mount and especially in the Beatitudes. We know it worked for him, and through all the centuries there has been hardly an adverse criticism of his life. We know it works for his followers. Every time we see a man who is gentle, humble, pure, brave for righteousness' sake, and merciful, it shines in his face. There is something about him that proclaims he has chosen the best things in life. In our best moments there is a driving desire to achieve those qualities for ourselves.

Havelock Ellis once remarked that the important thing is not to find a man who knows the answer to your problem, but to find a man who knows what the problem is. In Jesus we have one who knows both the problem and the answer to it. The problem is to find the kind of life that he describes as blessed. The answer is to sit at his feet until we have learned those qualities which he lists in the Beatitudes and which result in joy unspeakable and full of glory. If we can truly drink his cup and accept his authority, we shall learn how to be happy. With that high purpose let us accept the gracious invitation to the table of our Lord.

Continuing in Christ

J. WARREN HASTINGS

*For I have received of the Lord that which also I de-
livered unto you, That the Lord Jesus the same night in
which he was betrayed took bread: and when he had
given thanks, he brake it, and said, Take, eat: this is my
body, which is broken for you: this do in remembrance
of me. After the same manner also he took the cup, when
he had supped, saying, This cup is the new testament in
my blood: this do ye, as oft as ye drink it, in remembrance
of me, For as often as ye eat this bread, and drink this cup,
ye do shew the Lord's death till he come.*

—I Cor. 11:23-26

Hard by the church which I serve is a tavern. Perhaps a better name for it would be "joint." To it by day and
by night men and women go to partake of their favorite
alcoholic beverage and lounge in its vulgar atmosphere. It
is frequented by young and old alike. From the pavement
one can hear the strains of juke box music, the rattle of
bottle on glass, and the raucous laughter of its patrons.
Judging from the noise which emanates from the place the
conversations taking place within are loud and often
boisterous. Always a sense of pity seems to overwhelm me
as I pass the place, for I know that within its walls men
and women are searching for something, they know not
what. As I see them come forth, I know that their quest
for a fuller, finer life has not been successful. It takes higher

questing than that which goes on in a tavern to answer the deepest needs of men's hearts.

A very different reaction comes on Sunday mornings as I, with many others, partake of the emblems in the Communion service. Let me tell you what I witness from week to week.

Man is ever beset by a threefold problem, i.e., the mistakes, failures, and *inadequacies of the past;* the pressing problems and *bafflements of the present;* and the fears and *uncertainties of the future.* Beneath this threefold problem man has a passionate craving to bring his own personality to complete fulfillment. To succeed in the quest for a fuller life is the very essence of existence. To fail is continuous hell. In the Communion service he finds the answers to life's dilemmas and the peace that is beyond understanding.

Communion is a deep experience that enables an individual to see the past through the eyes of God. It means that something tremendous has been done for him, something that can and does add a glow of understanding and peace to all his yesterdays. He realizes afresh and with keen appreciation that Jesus Christ did and is doing something remarkable for man himself. The surrender that is the Lord's Table flows into man's very life. That faith in God which makes the sacrifice real becomes a part of the fiber of his soul. The attitude of humility that permeated the upper room is relevant for his own life. God was in that drama, and man knows it. Terrible as they were, his sins become blurred—almost forgotten—memories in the light of the love which "so loved the world" that it gave of its all in that first Lord's Supper. Man has a sense of forgiveness of sin as he partakes of the emblems.

The past is forever contiguous with the present. There

can be no present without a past. There must always be a past tense. Recently a father said to me, "I cannot live because of the sins of my past."

I replied, "You have done what you could to rectify the sins of days that are gone. You have called upon God for help. He will not fail you. His Son came into the world and gave himself that you might have life."

"Oh," he answered, "it was for others, not me."

"For you," I said, "broken for you. It is as though the Lord gave of his all for just you."

"But I am so unworthy," he replied.

"For you and you alone, who sinned so deeply, He gave all. The miracle of the Lord's Supper is that each repentant sinner knows that Christ suffered and died for even him."

The light was breaking across his countenance. His sinful past was lost in the sacrifice of the Son of God. It would never again be the millstone about his neck that it had been.

Carlyle said that a man is either a hero or a coward, and that is true. A stronger statement would have been, "Man is either understanding of the present, or he is not," because unless a person has a fairly sound understanding of the present, he is indeed lost. If life to him is an enigma, he has nothing upon which to lean in periods of stress. Either he has a wholesome philosophy of today's world, or he has not. There is no middle ground here.

This is a period that tries men's souls, breaks their wills, and frustrates their hopes. The temporalities in today's world are many. In relatively recent times we have seen four different types of government in Germany, three in France, three in Italy, two in Spain, two in Great Britain; and the list could be added to ad infinitum. One begins to wonder if there is anything permanent under the sun.

In the field of morals and pure idealism man is driven to say, "Change and decay in all around I see." A head nurse in the emergency ward of a hospital said, "Man is becoming expert in the wielding of a knife. We average five slashings a night." Man's disregard for man has reached a new high. His low esteem of his brother man, plus an almost complete void in the field of higher idealism, has led man to the brink of the precipice of failure and almost to the achievement of oblivion. He seeks an answer in the combination of gadgets that epitomize this age and comes away empty-hearted, if not empty-handed. There is no surcease from the cry of King Lear, "No man cares for my soul."

In the midst of chaos and despair man finds God's interpretation of life in the sweet quietness of the Communion Table. Here he discovers revelations that make life not only livable but lovely with a present glory. For the Lord's Supper takes place in the lives and hearts of men. Appearances to the contrary, God is still in the midst of life, "a very present help in trouble." One cannot experience life to the full if the only God he knows is an absentee landlord. God in life now is the greatest single concept he can possess.

Without this concept life remans a jigsaw puzzle that cannot be assembled into an intelligent whole. With it man can see "the finger of God moving in the affairs of humanity." He sees this as a moral, not an immoral universe. He sees the puny efforts of conceited men who try to build their cities and governments on other than a sound moral and ethical foundation collapse as a superstructure built on crumbling sand. He knows that man cannot break God's laws and enjoy the peace of righteous progress. He comes to the basic conclusion that "the wages of sin is death." When one realizes that God is active in today's world, he can see the divine handwriting on the so-called walls of civilization.

Continuing in Christ means a continuous revelation of God's presence in life. The experience of participating in the Lord's Supper does this for us.

The most frequent question that man asks is, "I wonder what the future holds for me?" That query is beneath many other questions that he asks. It reveals man looking into the unknown and terrifying future. Lecomte Du Noüy in his book *Human Destiny* discusses the long climb of man through the ages and says that man was content with living and procreating until the birth of conscience. He adds that from that moment man has been able to sleep peacefully only as he mastered himself—and that, I believe, includes a positive view of the future.

Fear is the most prevalent of all man's emotional reactions—fear of physical disease; of an enemy, imaginary or otherwise; of failure; or loss of reputation; of depression; of forces of evil; and often of life itself. Of all physical illnesses 80 per cent are grounded in mental and emotional attitudes, and the vast majority of them are rooted in fear. There can be no abundant Christian living in the midst of attitudes of fear. An answer must be found to the fear problem if life is to be livable.

The opposite of fear is righteous, intelligent hope, glorious faith, and inner peace. These are the attitudes that go to make up abundant living. He who has them is fortunate indeed, for he goes forth as life's master and not as its slave. It is in this area of thought and action that the religion of Christ makes all the difference in the world. It is here, in large measure, that the followers of Christ are different from other people. They have discovered a source for majestic living that no man can take from them. The finest achievement of God is a man or woman deep in the faith of Christ. The most inspiring individuals whom it has been my privilege to know have been persons of great faith in Jesus Christ, and because of that faith and their comprehension of his message they have been able to meet the future unafraid and full of hope.

At the Communion Table man finds himself looking into the unfoldings of the days ahead with faith and serenity because he realizes that the message of that table is eternal; he puts that message against life or, rather, sets it up in the midst of life. He realizes as he partakes of the emblems that God gave his only begotten Son that man might have abundant life. He knows that the forces of righteousness will ever, in the long run, conquer the powers of evil, that justice and truth are eternal. He knows that the message of Christ is true. Moreover, the realization comes to him with strong emphasis that the future, because of the love, power, and presence of God in Christ, is not something to be met in a spirit of fear. The future is in his hands, and man need not be afraid.

The accusation has been leveled against this age that it is not conducive to the development of spiritual power. We are, so the argument goes, so interested in things, so dependent upon gadgets, so trustful of human theories—and almost complete nervous wrecks with it all—that we have neither time nor inclination to listen to the "still small voice." There is much truth in this charge, but it does not tell the whole story.

Beneath the worries and troubles of his life a man must have a sense of peace and of the presence of divine power in order to live in a fair degree of abundance. "God moves

in a mysterious way his wonders to perform." As we participate in the Communion service, experiencing his blessings
in so many ways, this ultimate and final realization comes
into our lives: "It is God, in and through his Spirit, who is
actually working in my life. I have joined my forces to his
reservoir of power. I can carry on majestically because of his
nearness. I know that his Son is my Lord and Saviour."

Healing Hands

GASTON FOOTE

And he laid his . . . hand upon me.—Rev. 1:17

THROUGH AN OPEN WINDOW IN THE HOME OF JOHN MARK a gust of wind came from the southwest. The candles flickered on the long table, around which were seated Jesus and the twelve disciples. It was his last night on earth and the most climactic moment in the memorial supper. Twelve pairs of eyes were focused upon the face of the Master. With perfectly calm deliberation he was saying, "The hand of him that betrayeth me is with me on the table." Nothing he could have said would have shocked them more; an earthquake would not have been more startling. In this intimate group the Master knew that there were hands that would reach out to hurt him as well as hands that would tenderly remove his body from the cross.

It has ever been so. Where the spirit of Jesus Christ has gone, there have been hurtful hands as well as healing hands, betraying hands of diabolism as well as beloved hands of dedication, hands of Judas the betrayer as well as hands of John the beloved.

Let us consider first the misery that has been created in the world by these hurtful hands of Judas and his followers. Jesus was to experience within twenty-four hours the agony of the nails in hands and feet and the spear in his side—the result of the hurtful hands of the maddened mob. The crucifixion of God's Son, dramatized on Good Friday, is an eternal process; hurtful hands are ever seeking to shed innocent blood.

Last summer I stood within the walls of the old Colosseum of Rome and heard again some of the stories of the persecution of the early Christians. It was their faith in the living God that would not allow them to bend their knees and worship the emperor. Because of that faith the hurtful hands of the emperor's guards thrust them into the arena to be devoured by hungry animals. Could those stones but speak, what stories of heroism they would reveal. The hurtful hands of the world's Neroes have ever sought to choke the life out of Christendom.

Herodotus, the historian, tells us of "Infanticide Island" in the Tiber not far from the city of Rome. Mothers under cover of darkness would leave their unwanted babies there to be devoured on the following day by the vultures of the air or, even worse, to be taken by some exploiter who would cripple them and send them on the streets in later years to beg for coins which would be taken from them at the end of the day. According to Vaughn Wilkins in his book *And So Victoria* this sordid story of hurtful hands was repeated in England in the nineteenth century. Street waifs were kidnapped and by the barbaric method of child slavery forced to do the most despisable tasks for their taskmasters.

Harriet Beecher Stowe in her immortal *Uncle Tom's Cabin* focused the attention of the nation upon the injustice of the institution of human slavery. This was an overdrawn account and was not typical of the treatment of slaves at the hands of their master, but discriminating leaders of both the North and South are grateful for the abolition of the system of human bondage. To say the least, slavery legalized a system wherein the hurtful hands of men could choke the life out of their fellow men.

The hurtful hands of Judas are still with us. The landlord can still push his impoverished tenant to the wall. Shylocks can still exact their pound of flesh. Overworked and worried husbands can still, with or without the influence of alcohol, abuse their wives and children. You can read about it in the newspapers every day. Here is a hand, motivated by a heart of hate, that pulls the trigger and takes a life. Here is a lustful hand that reaches out and robs a girl of her purity, a hand that steals the life savings of a widow, the hand that strikes a child and makes it a cripple for life. These are the hands of Judas and his followers.

Consider now the tender ministries of those healing hands of the faithful disciples such as John and Andrew and Peter. Imagine, if you can, a Communion Table 25,000 miles long, reaching around the world. People of all races, colors, and creeds will be taking the holy cup, representing the shed blood of our Lord, and as they drink of it they will be reminded of the love of God for men everywhere. Think of all the people who will embrace this cup.

I am sure Dr. Stover of the Belgian Congo will touch this symbolic cup of our Lord. I met him in 1946 at the Leopoldville Missionary Conference. A native of Puerto Rico and of mixed blood, he had gone to the Congo almost fifty years ago as a missionary. Early one morning through the thin walls of the partition that separated our rooms I heard him praying. It was a prayer of agony. He was fervently praying that God would deliver his people from their indifference and give them a sense of divine mission. How he loved his people, and how they must have loved him! What beautiful hands he had, hands that caressed a newborn babe, hands that prayed God's blessings on a new convert, hands that helped a wounded comrade to his feet, hands with the healing of God in their finger tips. I am sure his hands will touch the cup.

I can imagine the hands of Dr. Schweitzer touching this symbolic cup of our Lord. What a healing ministry he has carried in those hands of his. He could have remained in Europe and with those talented hands released from the great cathedral organs the immortal music of Bach. But human need was too appalling in the river district of North Africa. He dedicated his hands as a medical missionary to the task of bringing physical, mental, and spiritual life to an abandoned people. No wonder that thousands of natives call him, in absolute reverence, the great white father. His hands helped heal their wounds, wiped tears from their eyes, and were a comfort to them in the hour of death.

In my imagination I can see the hand of that Chinese peasant in the little mission church reaching out to touch the cup. His wife starved to death early in the war. His oldest son was killed in battle. His daughter was captured and raped by enemy soldiers. All day long he foraged for food for himself and his small son and daughter at home. He refused to steal, to collect food under false pretenses, to engage in bribery. Through the years he trusted God, and he would rather die than compromise with his ideals. Somehow amid terrible odds he believed that God would see him through. I have never seen such faith in all of China as I saw in Tony Wong. Wherever he is, if he can find a church, his blessed hands will touch that cup.

I am quite sure that the hands of that German mother in Cologne will touch the cup of our Lord. She believed in honesty and purity, and had so taught her children. As she wiped the tears from her eyes, she told me her story. They had always had family prayer and had gone together as a

Healing Hands

family to church every Sunday. Then the powers of evil came into authority, and her children were taught that a nation should be physically strong even if it meant wreaking vengeance upon others. Government officials had insisted that her unmarried daughters should bear children for the fatherland. The day she defied the authorities they took her and her smallest child, a five-year-old, to the slave labor camp. Her husband and son had been killed in the war. The oldest daughter had not been heard from. After the war the mother and little girl, almost starved, came back home. But the home was not there. They could not even find a familiar stone amid the rubble. As I told them good-by, the mother said, "God will see us through." I have thought many times of that heroic mother and half-starved child. Somewhere I feel that the healing hands of that devoted mother have brought back life to the little child. Somewhere her hands will touch the cup.

When I was a lad of eleven years, I had a severe case of typhoid fever. My father was away at the time, and the doctor insisted that my father return home and care for me. The method of reducing the fever, six degrees above normal, was to give me cold baths. My father would take my warm feverish body and immerse me in cold water in an old zinc tub. It was a severe ordeal, and only the loving hands of a devoted father enabled me to endure it. The doctor said it was the healing hands of my father that carried me through. Were he yet living, I know his hands would be touching this cup of our Lord.

Bishop McCabe paid beautiful tribute to the devoted hands of his mother when he wrote:

I almost weep when looking back
To childhood's distant day;

ᴄᴠᴏ 171 ᴄᴠᴏ

And think how those hands rested not
When mine were at their play.

There are those hands whose form and hue
A sculptor's dream might be;
But mother's aged wrinkled hands
Are most beautiful to me.

Many are the hands throughout the world that touch the
cup on Communion Sunday. When we take the cup, we can
feel in imagination our own finger tips touching the finger
tips of millions of devoted hands dedicated to the healing
of the wounds of the world. We have hands that can bind
up broken wounds, give a crust of bread, lift a falling comrade. Let the healing hands of God touch our own hands
that they too may be healing hands. And as we touch the
cup, let it be a symbol of the dedication of our hands for the
healing of the nations.

Biographical Notes

JESSE M. BADER is the executive secretary of the Department of Evangelism of the Federal Council of Churches of Christ in America. A native of Illinois and a graduate of Drake University, he became secretary of evangelism for the Disciples Church in 1920 and came to the Federal Council in a similar position in 1934. During the last fifteen years he has been the leader in many national preaching missions from coast to coast.

ROY A. BURKHART has been minister of First Community Church, Columbus, Ohio, since 1935. He is president of the National Council of Community Churches and a member of the Board of Trustees of the International Council of Religious Education. Among his best-known books are *How the Church Grows* and *The Secret of a Happy Marriage*.

SAMUEL McCREA CAVERT has been general secretary of the Federal Council of Churches of Christ in America since 1921. Long identified with the ecumenical movements of the church, he was a member of the committee which drafted the plans for the World Council of Churches in Utrecht in 1938 and in Amsterdam in 1948. He was a member of the Board of Directors of the United Service Organizations during the war and of the Advisory Committee on Political Refugees.

CLARENCE TUCKER CRAIG is the dean of Drew Theological Seminary, Madison, New Jersey. He is one of the nine-member committee which published the Revised Standard Version of the New Testament and a contributor to the Amsterdam volume on *The Universal Church in God's Design*. Among his books are *The Beginning of Christianity, The Study of the New Testament,* and *We Have an Altar*.

HENRY HITT CRANE is minister of Central Methodist Church, Detroit, Michigan. A native of Illinois, he comes from five generations of Methodist preachers. Always in great demand as a speaker, he has spoken in more than 150 institutions of higher education throughout America. An indefatigable worker for world peace, he identifies himself with all movements related to better racial and industrial relationships in the turbulent city of Detroit.

EDWIN T. DAHLBERG has been minister of First Baptist Church, Syracuse, New York, since 1939. A graduate of Colgate-Rochester Divinity School, he was formerly president of the Northern Baptist Convention. He is a member of the Executive Committee of the Federal Council of

Churches and the Central Committee of the World Council of Churches.

F. GERALD ENSLEY is the minister of North Broadway Methodist Church, Columbus, Ohio. After graduating from Boston Theological Seminary in 1931 he remained there to teach homiletics and systematic theology until he moved to Columbus. He has given numerous lectures to college and university students throughout the Middle West.

GASTON FOOTE is the minister of Grace Methodist Church, Dayton, Ohio. A native of Texas, he has degrees from Southern Methodist University and Denver University. A world traveler, he attended the world conferences at Oxford, Edinburgh, Oslo, and Amsterdam. He is the author of several books, the latest being *The Words of Jesus from the Cross*.

ALFRED H. FREEMAN is the minister at First Methodist Church, Wichita Falls, Texas. A graduate of Southern Methodist University, he served churches in Oklahoma City and Corpus Christi, Texas. He attended the world church conferences in Oxford and Edinburgh in 1937 and was an official visitor at Amsterdam in 1948.

J. WARREN HASTINGS became the minister at the National City Christian Church, Washington, D. C., in 1942. A graduate of Yale Divinity School and the University of Edinburgh, he has served as minister in Savannah, Georgia, and Seattle, Washington. He carries on an aggressive ministry in perhaps the most strategic pulpit of his denomination.

CLYDE V. HICKERSON is the minister of the Barton Heights Baptist Church, Richmond, Virginia. He is a graduate of the University of Richmond and the Southern Baptist Seminary, Louisville, Kentucky. He is a contributor to many religious journals and is vice-president of the Baptist Foreign Mission Board.

ELMER G. HOMRIGHAUSEN is professor of Christian education at Princeton Theological Seminary, New Jersey. Educated at Princeton, Chicago University, and Rutgers, he is former professor of church history at Butler University, Indianapolis. He is a frequent lecturer in American seminaries and is chairman of the Department of Evangelism of the Federal Council of Churches. Among his books are *Let the Church Be the Church* and *Sermons by the Sea*.

G. RAY JORDAN is professor of preaching at Emory University, Atlanta, Georgia. He was educated at Duke University, and three former pastorates were at High Point, Winston-Salem, and Charlotte, North Carolina. A prolific writer, he contributes to numerous religious journals and periodicals. Among his recent books are *The Emerging Revival* and *The Hour Has Come*.